THE BUSINESS OF LEARNING

The Business of Learning

Staff and student experiences of further education in the 1990s

Patrick Ainley and Bill Bailey

CASSELL

Cassell
Wellington House
125 Strand
London WC2R 0BB

PO Box 605
Herndon
Virginia 20172

British Library Cataloguing-in-Publication Data
A catalogue record for this book is available from the British Library.

ISBN 0-304-33982-2 (paperback)
      0-304-33981-4 (hardback)

Designed and typeset by Kenneth Burnley in Irby, Wirral, Cheshire.
Printed and bound in Great Britain by Redwood Books, Trowbridge, Wiltshire.

Contents

Series introduction

It costs the taxpayer more than £2.5 billion a year, it provides work for more than 100,000 people and has two-and-a-half million clients. The workers are revolting, the customers are complaining, the police are investigating and 100 of its chief executives have suffered votes of no confidence. It is a big business in big trouble, but no one seems to care. Last week it was rocked by strikes and hardly anyone noticed.

We are talking about further education – the Cinderella service that caters for more of the over-16 population than all the schools and universities put together. Spread over 465 colleges, it provides everything from degree-level engineering to basic dressmaking. Yet FE is largely ignored by the media, which is a shame, because it is turning into a near war-zone.

Barry Hugill, 'Sleaze and loathing in the classes of conflict'
The Observer, 12 March 1995

This book is the first in a new series for which it seeks to set the tone. It aims to steer a middle course between academic studies on further education and the present predominant action research undertaken by management support agencies.

The latter type of action research, while it sets out to be of use *in* FE for implementation by managers to solve immediate problems, at its best represents a substantial but underdeveloped research effort where opportunities for theoretical advances for wider reflection and application are too often lost. At its worst, while often attractively packaged and presented, it seems – like much management literature in any area – rhetorical or platitudinous. Such research in FE is aimed mainly at managers, and relates but indirectly to the immediate concerns of lecturers in classrooms, laboratories and workshops, let alone to their students.

Academic research *on* FE, on the other hand, is often irrelevant to the sector's own concerns. This series therefore, unlike many others, will not be written by academics for academics. For there is some sensitivity in FE today about academic researchers 'coming down from on high' to investigate a sector of education in which they have previously had little interest; a sector moreover which is of such size and variety that it also aspires to conduct its own research as part of the degree-level teaching undertaken in many colleges. 'Don't patronize us', as Ruth Silver, the Principal of Lewisham College, warned the professor directing the Economic and Social Research Council's 'Learning Society Programme' when he proposed at a joint meeting with the Association for Colleges that the traditional universities, who had carved up the available research funds amongst themselves in the usual shameless manner, should conduct research on FE. The culture of research in FE to which the series will contribute would therefore be one in which teaching and research are not opposed and antithetical, as in the traditional universities, but complementary.

The series will therefore raise questions relating FE to wider changes in the economy and society, and analyse key developments in FE in relation to higher education and schools (particularly in the light of Sir Ron Dearing's proposals for schools, post-16 qualifications and HE) as well as to training. It will examine FE in a national and European perspective, as well as in comparison with the community colleges in the USA with which FE in the UK is often compared, and to similar arrangements for technical education in Australia, New Zealand and the Far East.

For reasons we outline in the first chapter of this book on the origins and history of further education in the UK, the whole FE sector is – with one or two notable exceptions – undertheorized. Anna Frankel and Frank Reeves, the authors of one of those rare exceptions, comment that, as well as a lack of theory – of ideas – 'The failure to fund a comprehensive programme of social science research into further education is nothing short of a national scandal'. Significantly, their book *The FE Curriculum* was published independently by their own college in 1996.

The idea of our book, like theirs, is to get people thinking and talking about what it is that they are doing in further education, whether they are teachers, students or managers; also, to address a wider readership outside of FE, too often ignorant of developments in the sector. We want to focus their attention and the debate over education and training on the future of FE as it becomes more uncertain.

Today, the sector is at a critical turning-point in its development. Arguably what happens to the 453 further education, tertiary and sixth-form colleges in England and Wales will determine the future direction of the whole of education as, with their more than three million full- and part-time students, the colleges are a crucial link between compulsory schooling and higher education as well as to post-compulsory learning in and out of employment. Certainly, the colleges have been recognized by government as central to the 'learning society' which is now agreed by all sides to be essential for future economic prosperity and social cohesion.

Discussions and decisions, however, need to be informed by evidence as well as ideas. The series which this book introduces is therefore also intended to contribute to a research culture in FE. In a newly incorporated sector there is an increasingly acknowledged necessity for colleges to research their own problems and practices. The former Further Education Unit (now part of the Further Education Development Agency) in 1993 called for 'a national debate on research in FE if the distinction and priority of research issues in FE is to be recognized'. The same year the Further Education Research Association held a conference on 'Creating a Research Culture in Further Education'. Similarly, the Association for Colleges' 1994 *Manifesto for Further Education* noted that 'in comparison with schools and the higher education sector, further education has not been a focus for strategic or operational research'. Since then little has been achieved. This is due as much to the immediate and critical problems facing further education colleges as to the lack of genuine interest in them from academic researchers.

Yet there are not many books on further education, even novels (compare the legion of novels about schools and universities with Tom Sharpe's *Wilt* from which the reading public derives its outdated image of the sector, only reinforced by a later film). Some of the reasons for this are explained in our Introduction. There are few good introductory books to the FE college system as a whole, one exception being Cassell's publication of Cantor, Roberts and Pratley's updated and expanded *A Guide to Further Education in England and Wales* (1995). Even this excellent work, by so comprehensively covering every aspect of the system, gives a misleading impression that the system is in fact systematic. This is certainly not how it is experienced by many of the students, teachers and managers working within it. It is upon their insights and experiences that we seek to base the books in this series.

Another book on FE that attempted such an approach was Gleeson, Mardle and McCourt's 1980 *Further Education or Training? A case study in the theory and practice of day-release education.* This set out to present 'what it is like for craft apprentices and their teachers to learn and teach within FE' (p. 7) and to make that experience travel to a wider readership. This series similarly sets out to communicate a feeling of 'what it is like', both for the teachers and the students, who share that experience and can build upon it, and to those in other sectors of education and in other public services, as well as to anyone who is concerned about the future shape and direction of society as a whole.

For it is important that the contemporary experience of further education is appreciated by a wider public, both the recent successes of the colleges and the present danger in which they find themselves. This critical situation is, we argue, the result of a funding system which has been instrumental in transforming further education since it was introduced in 1993. Now similar funding methods are under consideration for extension to schools, training and higher education. The new forms of funding and managing colleges are also very similar to means of running other public services in a welfare state that may soon be still further transformed out of all recognition.

It is urgent therefore that more people appreciate 'what it is like' and what is happening in the country's further education colleges. Their future is not a matter of academic debate, nor a question limited only to the economic well-being of UK PLC, or to the future of education and training to which FE makes such a vital contribution, but is – or should be – of vital political concern in deciding the future direction of our society as a whole. Our book and this series are a modest contribution to the informed and democratic debate which has to take place if we are to realize the human potential to learn from our experience in order to avoid the mistakes of the past and create a new future.

Introduction

If ther be anythyng that displese hem, I preye hem also that they arrette it to the defaute of myn unkonnynge, and nat to my wyl, that wolde ful fayn have seyd bettre if I hadde had konnynge.

Geoffrey Chaucer

This is a study of two colleges of further education. How 'representative' they, or any FE college, can be in a sector that is characterized by its variety, is discussed in Chapter 1. In a sense we could have picked any two colleges. The two that we did pick do at least illustrate the two main types of general and tertiary colleges funded by the Further Education Funding Council for England (FEFC), whose intricate and complex method of funding the colleges is explained in Chapter 2. We realize that our study is limited in its scope by being confined to only two colleges and we hope that the work that we have begun can be expanded upon and that other contributors to this series will broaden the paired case study with which we have started it off. However, the fact that our two colleges were so different – and yet, as will be seen, revealed some essential similarities – relates to one of the central themes of this book.

For one of the questions that this book raises is: how appropriate is a funding system that in principle proposes to fund equally every student on the same course and in the same circumstance at every college in the country? As we shall see, this new funding method appeared the most equitable possible. Indeed, it has been proposed as a model for funding higher, as well as further education, students and for extension to all students and trainees in schools and on schemes at all ages. In the words of a leaked Treasury memo (publicly dismissed by then-Chancellor Kenneth Clarke):

> To change the balance of funding between taxpayer and other beneficiaries and to inject more market mechanisms into the delivery of education and training, funding institutions may be replaced by financing individuals with vouchers, grants, loans and employer contributions.

We raise questions about the actual functioning of the FEFC's funding method and its consequences as shown in the two colleges. We hope that this will contribute to the debate on the future of funding, not for only FE, but also for other education, training and public services. For such sweeping proposals as the above have not gone away, whichever party may be in power. Also, while the Dearing reviews of '16–19 Qualifications' and of higher education may have – temporarily perhaps – artificially separated the intimately connected higher and further education sectors, such solutions to funding for all post-compulsory learning (including schools) remain attractive to sections of both the main Parliamentary parties.

Our two colleges, if not representative, are indicative of the two main types of college in the FE sector – the generalist and the tertiary colleges. Different possibilities are open to them in the new further education and training market, the creation of which we briefly describe in our opening chapters. The response to these changes by students and staff at the two colleges is then illustrated in subsequent chapters, with particular emphasis on the similarities and differences between the comments received from the two groups at the colleges. For the two colleges can, we conclude, also be taken as suggestive of a possible future for further education. This future is more than ever uncertain and we intend our conclusions and suggestions as contributions to a debate on what should happen that is long overdue.

One consequence of the new independence of FE colleges as semi-private but still largely state-funded corporations competing for the business of learning is that co-operation between them, save in a minority of exceptional cases, has become increasingly problematic and rare. For colleges are loath to pass on information and expertise to others, including schools and training agents, who are now perceived as their local competitors. This affects research on FE, especially if it is undertaken on a local or regional basis – as arguably it needs to be. Our two colleges were in very different localities, socially and geographically, and this too adds to the contrast between them, accentuating the question of why they should be funded equally. But, as one of our two Principals said in interview: 'I need a distance of at least 50 miles before I can actually start talking really honestly about this place . . . I have virtually minimal contact now with my colleagues in other colleges locally because we're desperately competitive.'

By describing these two very different colleges we also illustrate the range of provision in the sector for general readers who may be unaware of its size and importance, or whose perceptions are limited to education being synonymous with schools, as appears to be the case in most political debate. In the discussion about the way forward for schools, as much as in the less extensive debate over the future of higher education and also of training, further education cannot be ignored as it has been too often in the past. This book is a small contribution to raising its political and public profile.

Hopefully the means we have adopted to undertake the description of two FE colleges in this book, a method which one of the two authors has developed and refined over a series of studies since 1986, serves to capture and convey the quality of the experience it seeks to contain and so gives readers a feeling of what it is like to study and teach in FE today. We hope that it will both inform those outside the sector and resonate with the experiences of those within it. In both cases we intend the book and the series it introduces to stimulate debate and theoretical argument into an area of education that is undertheorized.

For this is not a study that contrasts the two colleges in terms of any comparative analytical framework enabling them to be compared in relation to independent variables, or any such supposedly 'objective' and semi-quantitative and statistical approach. Instead, the method adopted was primarily qualitative – based on interviews with participants at all levels of learning, from Foundation-level students to Principals, in the two colleges. This qualitative approach recognizes with Winch (1958) the futility of trying to give a single 'objective' description and so proceeds by an account that is, as much as possible, expressed in the words of participants themselves. We can say that at its simplest our approach recognizes that to aid understanding two heads are better than one, three are better than two and so on. So the idea is to speak to as many people as possible to build up a picture of what is going on and how they experience it.

Generally such an approach works to produce agreement that from a number of perspectives illuminates what is actually occurring. However, in this case we found that at both colleges we were getting a very different impression of events from the managers and the students that we spoke to, compared with the accounts given to us by the teachers at both places. The former are recounted in Chapters 3 and 5 and the latter in Chapter 4. This was evident to such an extent that little agreement appeared possible between these groups about what was actually happening in either place. This set us a puzzle to explain the variation in the two versions of events without actually denying the validity of one of them. Happily, such an explanation as is put forward in Chapter 6 was afforded by the theoretical explanation we had ourselves advanced to explain the recent history of further education which was presented in Chapters 1 and 2. That it could explain the variation in the two accounts by managers and, to a lesser extent, by students on the one side, and, on the other, by teachers, convinced us of its validity.

We put it forward here as a contribution to debate on the quality and future of further education to which it relates and indeed to the future of education and training as a whole.

Acknowledgements

To all the staff and students at the two colleges in this study, especially to their two Principals who made the study possible and their Deputies and Assistants who so efficiently expedited it.

Also to Ken Glanfield at Tower Hamlets College, Jane Hemsley-Brown now of Southampton University, John Offord in the Research Office of the National Union of Students, Professor John Pratt of East London University, Peter Robinson at the London School of Economics, Claire Wallace, and Sir Toby Weaver C.B.

And to all our colleagues at the University of Greenwich School of Post-Compulsory Education and Training, especially Harriet Harper, Linda Haworth, Professor John Humphries, Diana Jones, Geoff Stanton and Judith Watson.

Naomi Roth at Cassell and her assistants, David Barker and Seth Edwards.

Ainleys and Baileys.

Chapter 1

Where the colleges came from and what they are

Further education has been, and to a surprisingly large extent still is, the best-kept secret in our education system.

Colin Flint, Principal, Solihull College

Where the colleges came from

There are now 453 colleges – 222 further education and 66 tertiary colleges, and 110 sixth-form colleges, plus 32 agricultural, 9 art, design and performing arts colleges and 14 other 'specialist designated institutions'. Together these receive public funding to the tune of nearly £3 billion a year from the Further Education Funding Council for England. Most of this money pays nearly a quarter of a million full- and part-time employees – 60 per cent of whom are teaching staff. The smallest colleges have fewer than 500 students and the largest over 20,000. They have over three million students altogether, predicted to rise by a quarter of a million a year to an anticipated four million by the year 2000. The majority of them are adults, 54 per cent are women and 65 per cent part-time.

Most of these students are in the FE and tertiary colleges, only seven per cent in the sixth-form colleges and another six per cent in other specialist colleges. Altogether they make up more than twice as many students as all the full- and part-time students at universities and other colleges of higher education, and more is spent on them than on all higher education. In addition, there are perhaps another 600,000 students in around 3,000 private FE institutions outside the state sector. These institutions tend to concentrate on English language learning, computing and business studies, and they are mainly located in the south east of England. Despite all this, many people remain totally ignorant about what further education colleges are and where they came from.

All these colleges have different origins. Many are long-established institutions whose origins can be traced to the late nineteenth century when concern about foreign competition and local pride in industrial achievement led to the establishment of municipal technical colleges in many industrial towns and cities. Some were established in the last 30 years. Others are the product of mergers of two or more colleges, for example of specialist, formerly monotechnic organizations which concentrated upon art, building or another craft.

The impressive facades of many of the older colleges often mask an unintegrated architecture of corridors and classrooms, workshops, lecture halls and laboratories –

'typical whisky-money buildings', as Chuter Ede, Parliamentary Secretary to the Board of Education during the Second World War, once described them. 'Whisky money' was the duty raised on beer and spirits in 1890 and passed to local councils with a recommendation that a suitable purpose for it was to aid the provision of technical instruction. This is all that anyone seems to remember of the history of technical and further education. It reveals the aspiration to bring education to the masses, 'distilling enlightenment out of whisky and beer', as Sydney Webb said at the time. In this elevated intention, the municipal colleges followed upon the tradition of the voluntarily founded Mechanics Institutes of the first half of the nineteenth century from which some of them grew. As we shall see, this tradition of municipal public service lives on in the colleges.

Few people, however, understand the work of further education colleges even today, despite their imposing presence in so many town centres. The growth of college enrolments beyond their traditional clientele of skilled manual workers, nearly all men, is only a recent development. This means that despite the large numbers now involved, relatively few people have experience of further education historically, and this appears to be particularly the case for groups involved in policy-making for the sector. This ignorance is not helped by the jargon of technical and further education, these days aggravated by acronyms and abbreviations incomprehensible to many, but which we will also find ourselves using. There is, for example, a jungle of qualifications and examining bodies. Also, teachers in FE have the title of lecturers, which can be daunting and off-putting to the unconfident prospective student. So can grand titles, like 'College of Further and Higher Education' or 'College of Art and Technology'. For, despite this high-falutin' terminology, the basic work of the colleges has always been the teaching of the theory and practice of the skills used in everyday occupations – in branches of engineering, office work, building and the particular industries of different parts of the country.

Not that the 'college' nomenclature of a higher status education was wholly irrelevant, for some colleges ran courses for external degrees of London University. They then used this experience to 'drift' academically, as Tyrrell Burgess and John Pratt originally put it, but also socially towards the university sector. Enabling the 'unfriended talent' of individual working-class students to get on was the glory of traditional FE. Yet the colleges shared with their successful students, who completed arduous courses of technical instruction, the tendency to raise their social status by moving away from the practical, technical and scientific by associating themselves with the generally applicable and bookish knowledge of management and the professions reached through academic specialization. In the same way that many of today's universities disguise their humble origins in colleges of art and technology, FE students often qualified themselves to get on in life by moving off the shop floor and into the office. Today many colleges offer degrees by franchise from universities, so that a quarter of a million of their students progress within their walls to degree-level and beyond.

Nevertheless, further education's existence on the margins of English and Welsh education has come about through the absence of public policy to plan the provision of post-school education and training. Even though what was to become the Board of Trade first began funding technical education in Schools of Design as long ago as 1836, there has never been any effort to identify and provide a national minimum of courses for young workers and adults. Or, more accurately, there was no implementation of legislation for such a national system. The Education Acts of 1918 and 1944, for instance, included sections requiring all school-leavers to continue in part-time education and training up to the age of 18 but in neither case were these proposals implemented.

So the history of FE is also part of a larger apparent indifference towards generations of young people, the majority of whom had no further formal education after leaving school. This neglect of most young workers is related to another aspect of the failure to replace traditional apprenticeships with a modern system of technical and vocational training before or during employment. Instead, there was from the early 1900s an increase in public and official interest in the debilitating effects of industrialism upon young people. This concern centred on the social, physical and moral effects upon young men – particularly of what used to be called 'blind-alley' or 'dead-end' jobs and, increasingly, of prolonged periods of unemployment. From the Boer War onwards, recurrent moral panics surrounded these working-class youngsters as future citizens, soldiers, parents and workers who might lose their 'work ethic' as the devil found work for their idle hands.

Such panics were explained at the time in terms of the newly invented concept of adolescence. Any remaining national interest in the systematic vocational training of young people was replaced by a moral crusade to rescue, civilize and school youth for its future place in society. From representing the nation's hopes for the future, the young came to be seen as a threat to the established order. The intention was to draw working-class youngsters in particular into a unified national experience. Insofar as this persistent cultural concern found any effective expression in schools and elsewhere, it hampered the development of an integrated education system bringing together the academic and vocational to contribute to technical and political modernization.

Characteristic of a system separating education from training was a division of responsibility for 'schemes' and 'initiatives' to deal with the young and adult unemployed under the former Ministry of Labour/Department of Employment from the Department of Education's main responsibility for schools. With each economic recession these rivalries resurfaced, so that in the 1930s, for instance, the Labour Ministry ran Government Training Centres in the Special Areas while local education authorities were given money to establish Juvenile Instruction Centres for unemployed youth. In the recessions after 1973, conflict between these two Ministries of State was a consistent theme of the troubled contemporary history of education and training.

All this means that in England and Wales – unlike in many other developed countries – there was until recently no national pattern in the provision of further education. Even today, with a centralized and regulated framework in which colleges compete on costs equalized through a national funding method and with national quality standards and inspection, there is still no national plan for FE. And although there is now a unified Department for Education and Employment, training remains the responsibility of employers through local Training and Enterprise Councils (Local Enterprise Companies in Scotland).

Neither have the FE colleges been recognized as part of the mainstream education system. FE is therefore still described negatively as neither schooling on the one hand nor higher education on the other; or – still more dismissively and inaccurately – as 'non-academic', being concerned solely with vocational training rather than general education. The result of this history of neglect and marginalization is that there has never been any agreed and generally understood assertion of the value of FE in its own right. It was only in 1996 that a single national lobby group for FE (the Association of Colleges) was established, one of its purposes being to make the sector's presence felt in national educational debates. FE remained a local affair at most until very recently. Its achievements went unsung and were disconnected from developments in the national system of schools and higher education.

As with so much else in England, this lack of status has much to do with social class; through its origins and associations further education was almost by definition for working-class students. Their education was vocational with the application of learning for practical paid employment plainly in view. Compared with sixth-form study, which offered possibilities of progression to higher education, training for a skilled job at the local 'tech' has always been seen as a second-best, an inferior option. This has been reflected in the perspectives and priorities of politicians, national and local, throughout the twentieth century. Given the weakness of pressure from groups within further education, or the industries for which colleges trained skilled workers, the focus of public policy has been mainly on the extension and the organization of compulsory schooling.

FE has also been affected by the fact that the development of a national system of schooling took place late in comparison with other European countries. This is because the provision of further and technical education can take place only when effective compulsory schooling has established the necessary foundation of basic skills and general knowledge. Such a full-time elementary education to age 14 only became the general rule in England and Wales after 1918. It was not until after the Second World War that secondary education for all to age 15 became established. The school-leaving age was raised again by a further year to 16 in 1972.

Schools policy has dominated the educational debate during the post-war period. This began with the move away from the tripartite system of selective grammar, technical and secondary modern schools, set up in 1944 as part of the settlement of the welfare state. This move away from secondary selection was based on a critique not least of its failure to develop the 'human capital' needed by a modern economy. When this structural change to comprehensive secondary schools accelerated during the 1970s, official concern turned at last to the needs of those who left school at the age of 16. The context for this broadening of focus was the end of the long economic boom following the oil price rise of 1973. With the re-emergence of unemployment, in particular among school-leavers, the Manpower Services Commission, a quasi-autonomous governmental organization, was set up by the Department of Employment under the Heath government. The aim of this organization was to modernize training and employment measures. It therefore began to direct ear-marked funding at schemes for unemployed 16–18-year-olds and for adults. The majority of these schemes consisted of work experience on employers' premises lasting for one year.

This initiative coincided with a demographic bulge in the 16–19 age group which tended to strengthen the trend towards increased voluntary staying-on at school or college beyond the new statutory leaving age of 16. Higher achievement by many youngsters in comprehensive schools, the majority of whom now gained qualifications for the first time, reinforced this tendency. Yet it became increasingly difficult for even qualified leavers to get jobs and the 1974–79 Labour government found itself paying more and more for make-work schemes as rising unemployment proved a permanent and not, as was thought at first by most economists, a temporary and cyclical problem.

After 30 years of full employment when school-leavers could be sure of finding work, it was clear that the situation facing those who left school at the earliest opportunity to go into jobs without any formal further education or training – up to this point always the majority of young people – was changing fundamentally. Apprenticeships to skilled employment were also collapsing with the decline of traditional heavy industries. So by the late 1970s, 16-year-olds approaching the end of their secondary schooling had the alternatives of staying on full time at school or college, leaving for employment which might or might not involve further education and training, joining the YOP (the Youth Opportunities Programme, as the scheme for unemployed school-leavers was called from 1977), or being on the dole.

Deepening recession, rising unemployment and the demographic bulge in school-leavers forced the education and training of the 16–19 age group upon the attention of politicians and the local and central education authorities. Discussion centred upon the range of courses available at 16-plus – a range which could be categorized as academic (A-level), vocational (traditional technical qualifications) and training or work experience for the unemployed. These types of provision had different origins, were the responsibility of different government departments and were funded in different ways. When only a minority of the age group were affected, such anomalies could be ignored or, from another point of view, valued as matters of choice and diversity. As more were involved, the differences between these alternative routes – their aims, content and funding – came to be seen as in need of harmonization.

Debates over post-compulsory education and training were informed by comparison of English provision with that of other countries. As connections were made between educational performance and economic progress, the UK's provision came to be seen as relatively underdeveloped and dysfunctional. The German 'dual system' of education and training was then particularly attractive to both the Labour government, the trade unions and to employers' organizations like the Confederation of British Industry. In Germany at that time the majority of school-leavers went at age 16 into high-quality training in companies which provided practical instruction combined with theoretical instruction at vocational schools, while a minority remained at school to prepare for entry to professional level higher education.

In 1976, James Callaghan, the Labour prime minister, initiated a so-called 'Great Debate' on education with his speech at Ruskin College in Oxford. Alongside leading employers who were laying off workers rather than retraining them, Callaghan now blamed schools, teachers and young people themselves for youth unemployment because they were inadequately prepared for work. Perhaps through its repetition, this unsubstantiated argument came to be widely accepted and vocational relevance to the needs of industry came to replace the principle of equal opportunities for all as the purpose of state schooling.

Mrs Thatcher as prime minister was to translate Labour's old electoral slogan into opportunities to be unequal, although during the 1980s a series of White Papers proposed modernizing training and increasing the responsiveness of schools and colleges to the needs of industry. 'A New Training Initiative' was launched in 1981, for example, and 'The Education and Training of Young People' followed in 1985. The MSC's Technical and Vocational Education Initiative, announced in 1982, also attempted to create a more vocationally relevant curriculum in schools and colleges. In introducing these and other programmes – notably the one-year Youth Training Scheme, introduced in 1983 to replace the YOP and extended to two years in 1985 – the MSC pioneered forms of dedicated funding that were bid for by local education authorities and other managing agents. In 1986 the Department of Employment established the National Council for Vocational Qualifications to erect a framework of vocational certification. This came to be based upon the 'competences' identified by employers for the performance they required in their various industries.

It was no accident that so many of these initiatives were undertaken by the Department of Employment rather than the Department of Education. Fundamentally, without the full employment policy that had underpinned Keynesian demand management of the welfare state, the Employment Department had nothing to do except provide relief for the two to three million rendered redundant at any one time by permanent and structural unemployment throughout most of the 1980s. The Employment Department, therefore, sought to take over education as its raison d'être. At one stage it almost succeeded in doing so, but in the end Education won out after the employment and training services of the old Employment Department had been taken over by local employer-run Training and Enterprise Councils/Local Enterprise Companies. What was left of the Employment Department that did not go to either the Department of Trade and Industry or to Social Security was then subsumed into a new Department for Education and Employment (DfEE) in 1995. Despite the confusions of these inter-departmental rivalries, exacerbated by factional in-fighting in the ruling Conservative Party, the 1970s and 1980s can be seen as the first decades during which central government policies began to impact upon the FE colleges.

From the 1970s onwards governments of both parties had attempted to control and reduce public expenditure so that local authorities came under pressure to reduce their costs. In some areas this led to the establishment of tertiary colleges which normally would be the sole provider of courses of all kinds to all those over the age of 16 living in a particular area. Sometimes this rationalization of provision was adopted as part of a move to extend comprehensive provision to a tertiary level. The incoming Conservative government in 1979 began an inquiry into this aspect of 16–19 provision that resulted in the Macfarlane Report of 1981. The conclusion in the first draft of this report recommended that, for educational and cost reasons, tertiary colleges should be adopted as official policy. This recommendation was deleted at the highest level and this represents a lost moment for the colleges which were from then on left in competition with school sixth forms.

The process of going tertiary had begun with Exeter way back in 1970. As Caroline Benn and Clyde Chitty point out in their recent history of comprehensive education, these tertiary colleges were created specifically to promote the development of comprehensive education rather than to merely rationalize A-level provision (like the sixth-form colleges) or offer a limited range of work-related qualifications (like many FE colleges at the time). As with the move to comprehensive schools, Conservative-controlled authorities often led the way, as many were in mainly rural areas with small sixth forms and under-used colleges. By 1992 there were 57 tertiary colleges with 90,000 full-time 16–19-year-old students. There was, however, less possibility of such tertiary reorganization in the large Labour-controlled cities, partly because some parents and most school teachers fought to preserve their sixth forms and partly because many Labour councillors, who were committed to comprehensives, thought of these as 11–18 schools with sixth forms, like grammar schools. Even in those places, like Sheffield and Manchester, where Labour councils reorganized provision at 16-plus, the move to a tertiary system was incomplete as some schools were able to retain their sixth forms, later threatening to opt out if they were not allowed to keep them. The opportunity was thus lost to bring further education colleges into the mainstream state education system by carrying forward the comprehensive reform of secondary schooling to a tertiary level, normalizing the transition from school at 16 to full- or part-time attendance by all school-leavers along with many adults in their local FE college.

Beyond the usual concentration of concern upon state schooling, policy debate occasionally visited higher education. In 1963 the Robbins Report led to the foundation of the new universities and the elevation of the Colleges of Advanced Technology to university status. Other colleges were later collected together and augmented to create the polytechnics (Central Institutions in Scotland). They were intended to provide opportunities for graduate level and other advanced study for people living in the areas that came under the control of the local authorities that ran the colleges. Arguably however, the binary division between the polytechnics and universities generated and sustained – in higher education as elsewhere – a simplified opposition between academicism and vocationalism, education and training, generalized knowledge and vocational competence. There was, though, something of a national debate about this with enthusiasts advancing the cause of the polytechnics as 'The People's Universities', creating what Eric Robinson saw as 'a comprehensive system of education for adults' to replace 'the concept of the boarding school university by that of the urban community university'.

The 1992 Further and Higher Education Act, which ended the binary division between polytechnics and universities, also lumped together FE, tertiary and sixth-form colleges as a discrete sector of incorporated colleges. Previously, under Section 41 of the 1944 Education Act, further education was defined very widely as any 'full-time and part-time education' and/or 'leisure-time occupation, in . . . organized cultural training and recreative activities' for 'persons over compulsory school age'. Yet, in the pronouncements and promises of most politicians and pundits, education still means compulsory education, i.e. 'schools'. When the use of the word 'education' is occasionally stretched in public debate to include non-compulsory learning, it reaches only to nursery schools or sometimes universities but rarely to further education colleges.

What they are – inside your local college today

From what we have already said of the origins of the colleges it is evident that every generalization about further education needs immediate qualification. There is, therefore, no such thing as a typical college. As a consequence of the way colleges grew up, closely related to their localities, different local populations of students have been served by quite different ranges of college provision. So, if you stop to look inside any college of further education today, you will discover a wide range of courses with a variety of work being undertaken by a disparate body of students taught by lecturers with many different educational backgrounds and life experiences. The answer therefore to the question 'What does a college do and what is it for?', is many things.

The Further Education Funding Councils divide the colleges they fund into three broad types – FE and tertiary, sixth-form and specialist. It can be argued that the differences between them are breaking down. The small sixth-form colleges are especially under pressure, if they cannot become more academic, to merge with the larger further or tertiary colleges. As Professor Peter Scott in his authoritative survey (1996) of *The Meanings of Mass Higher Education* records,

> For almost a quarter of a century FE colleges have been engaged in a long revolution, sloughing off their technical school past and evolving towards a broader community-wide comprehensive college future (their trajectory is uncannily reminiscent of that followed by the former polytechnics). As long as they were local authority institutions, the depth of this transformation was partly obscured by the persistence of political localisms. (page 52)

Nevertheless, he also says that within the FE sector as a whole there still exist 'more than a hundred mini-sectors', that is as many as there are local authorities.

Certainly, for at least the past 30 years, further education has been growing largely unnoticed, not only in terms of student numbers but also in the breadth of the courses on offer to them. The traditional work of colleges was always vocational courses leading to technical qualifications that related to the students' work. These were not just for the young men on day- and block-release courses, who had for long been the staple fare of the old technical colleges. The colleges also responded to demand for and from growing numbers of young women who began to attend college. The majority of them wanted courses that prepared them for work in the expanding office sector of employment or in health and social care.

Yet, vocational education of one sort or another is still 'the core business' of further education, as college Principal Mike Austin called it in the *Times Educational Supplement* (8 March 1996), 'the preparation of people for a working life in all the professions, trades and vocations'. Today nearly four out of every five qualifications achieved by college students are vocational. These can be for jobs students have or jobs they hope to get. It can be for qualifications to be used for a specific job or occupation (nowadays National Vocational Qualifications), or a qualification related to a broader area of employment (for instance, City and Guilds of London Institute Certificates, Business and Technology Education Council Certificates and Diplomas, or General

National Vocational Qualifications – applied A-levels as they were once supposed to be called).

A second category of work that is nowadays larger than vocational education in many colleges is that of academic education, often having grown out of the general education or liberal studies supplementary to the vocational provision above. During the 1950s, but especially in the 1960s, colleges began to provide full- and part-time classes leading to GCE O- and A-levels for 15–16-plus-year-olds who did not have the opportunity for them in their secondary modern schools, or who had decided to move to the college for a more adult atmosphere. Adult returners to learning also took advantage of these classes so that many colleges began to serve as alternative sixth forms for 16–18 and older students. For some of these students the colleges were providing a second chance after poor results at schools. For others, it was in fact their first chance. Continuing unplanned growth over the past 30 years has led to the situation where there are today more A-level students in the FE sector than in school sixth forms.

Over the same period, FE colleges also provided programmes for school-leavers with 'special educational needs'. Until the 1970s there was little provision for young people over 16 and adults with physical disabilities and/or learning difficulties. Previously, they were often cared for by their parents or in training workshops with no further education. Or, if they worked in the routine and repetitive jobs then thought appropriate for them, they were the first to feel the pinch as automated new technology led to the elimination of much unskilled labour. Following the 1978 Warnock Report, students with statements of special educational need increasingly graduated from school to FE. The provision for these students still remains patchy, however, with some colleges taking many 'students with learning difficulties and/or disabilities', as they are now called, while others take few. As with schools, extra funding can be claimed for students needing additional support so that some schools and colleges concentrate upon them while others choose to place their emphasis elsewhere, on academic courses for instance, if not trying to provide for everyone in an inclusive manner.

As rising and permanent unemployment began to exclude growing numbers of young people newly entering the labour market from paid work of any sort, students with special educational needs were joined by other school-leavers in 'multiskills workshops' on Youth Training Schemes. Many colleges managed YT Schemes, once again keeping themselves afloat and meeting changing demands as their traditional vocational provision declined. With increasing unemployment, colleges also provided training for unemployed older people on a succession of other schemes. While many of these training programmes were temporary stop-gaps, there was also basic, as well as occupationally specific skills provision intended to help people obtain jobs. By 1995 an Association for Colleges survey found 100,000 unemployed people studying part-time under the so-called 21-hour (now reduced to 16-hour) rule. This rule enabled the students to continue to claim unemployment benefit or the latest Jobseekers' Allowance while remaining technically 'available for work'.

In addition, in many areas where local authority provision has been squeezed, the colleges are now the only providers of traditional non-vocational classes for adults; for example, in subjects like local history, cake decoration, foreign languages for the holidaymaker, or tea-dance clubs for pensioners. The colleges also supply English language learning to immigrants, refugees and asylum seekers, as well as to foreign visitors to the UK. In several colleges these language courses and other programmes are provided also to students abroad through 'distance learning' by correspondence or via videos and the internet. Like the Open University with its 157,450 students worldwide, some colleges have begun to use new communication and information technologies to deliver distance learning to students.

Courses are also provided to employees on employers' premises in the private and public sector, along with professional development programmes for managers and others. Employers often negotiate contracts with local colleges for the provision of customized courses for their employees. These courses often coincide with companies' moves into new markets, the introduction of new products and services, or when introducing new technology and work reorganization. Community groups also use college premises or franchise what the Further Education Funding Council calls 'outward collaborative provision' in their local centres or even in students' homes.

Finally, access courses for adults – many of them unemployed – have recently become a significant part of college provision. Sometimes as part of Open College networks or federations, these are usually undertaken in co-operation with local universities, especially former polytechnics. They provide introductions to learning which, if completed successfully, lead into degree courses, full- or part-time. Large parts of first degree programmes, as well as other higher education qualifications, such as Higher National Diplomas, may also be provided by colleges on franchises from universities and other higher education institutions. Already nearly half of all colleges are franchisers of parts of degree courses or run access programmes for higher education institutions. In fact, 13 per cent of all HE level students are in FE. This is more than the total of HE students in HE itself before the expansion of the new universities following the 1963 Robbins Report. In 1993–94 the Higher Education Funding Council for England allocated £26 million in recurrent grant for teaching 32,000 students on graduate, degree and sub-degree courses in 76 FE colleges. In addition, the HEFCE funds another 27,000 student places currently franchised to colleges and validated by either universities or national validating bodies such as BTEC (now EDEXCEL). Most of these access and franchise courses are much cheaper to run in FE than HE. Nevertheless, despite increased demand from mainly local and mature students unable or unwilling to travel away to university, seven out of ten colleges have been forced to cut or abandon degree and diploma courses, according to the Association for Colleges reported in the *Times Educational Supplement* (27 January 1995). For the future of these new co-operative ventures has been put in doubt by government cut-backs in previous high projections for HE student numbers announced at the end of 1993. However, the two inter-related sectors of further and higher education have been included together, legislatively at least, for the first time in the title of the 1992 Further and Higher Education Act.

No other sector of education in this country has diversified its offer of courses in order to serve such a wide range of students. While a few universities have as many students as some large colleges, their course offer is nowhere near as diverse or as complicated to manage. It is this diversity that makes for the unclear public perception of FE. This issue of focus, or rather the lack of it, is important in the English system of education which recognizes and values clarity of purpose and accords high status to clear-cut categories and single-purpose institutions. Further education colleges, as we have seen, are not so simple. They do not make comprehension easy for those attempting to understand their workings for the first time.

What is clear amongst all the changes of recent years is that the old English or Welsh tech or night school, attended mainly by young male workers in the evening or on day release, has long gone. In place of their concentration upon engineering and building, which the Crowther Report on '15 to 18' noted in 1959, colleges of further education are now general purpose institutions of education and training for people above the school-leaving age. They have become multipurpose institutions – open, community service stations, with full- and part-time students split across many sites. In enlarging their role – in the absence, it must be said, of any official policy or definition to which they could work – the colleges were meeting their own needs for institutional survival and growth as well as those of the students they enrolled. Their scope for development, of course, varied from area to area, depending on the local form of secondary reorganization, the variety and fortunes of local industries and relations with local institutions of higher education. As usual, the colleges were pulled all ways but also related more directly than schools and most HE to training for and in work. With this diversity of aims, in the new market in education and training it is unclear who exactly the clients of FE are – whether individual students, their parents, employers, or their local communities.

All this growing provision was and is attended voluntarily. Even with the removal of state benefits from 16–18-year-olds leaving unemployed youngsters no option but the Youth Training allowance on schemes often run in colleges, there has been and still is no legal requirement to attend. This absence of implementation of compulsory attendance also contributes to patchy provision by colleges – literally of places – in local areas. Consequently, there are more college places in some areas than in others and there is no guaranteed minimum of provision in further education.

The colleges' position is in clear contrast with that of schools and, as a result, colleges have always had to attract business in the form of students to their courses and programmes. In turn, this means that they have always to some extent had to operate in a competitive market. As Professor Denis Gleeson explained in a journal article, 'private enterprise and market forces in FE are not a new phenomenon'. 'Indeed,' he continued:

> . . . the ethos of contemporary FE is rooted in its voluntaristic and entrepreneurial traditions. Unlike the growth of mass schooling, FE has taken a highly individualistic path, its expansion depending much on the patronage of industry, business and commerce and the ability to attract greater student numbers.

Neglect by central government meant that colleges had to take their own routes and devise their own futures. FE teachers and managers were left to get on with their business as they saw fit, unhindered by central state interference. Positive in some ways, as Gleeson points out, this also produced a 'curriculum development reflecting anomalies in both the labour market and qualifications jungle . . . replication, duplication and waste'.

For Conservative traditionalists, however, FE offers a model of how schools and universities also ought to be – unplanned and therefore, so it is argued, unbureaucratic and immediately responsive to the demands of their local customers whether they be parents, students or neighbouring employers. In serving the latter in particular, such a vision of the colleges as the 'Handmaidens of British Industry' only perpetuates FE's outdated, technical, night-school and part-time, supplementary image inherited from the past. It obscures the transformations that have occurred in recent years, both to British industry and to FE, especially the growth of a whole new constituency of new types of full-time students.

The story of the colleges, though, is not one of individual enterprise triumphing against official neglect, for it was the attitude and support of the local education authorities with regard to FE that was the largest influence on colleges' development. Under the 1944 Education Act the LEA's statutory duty was to provide facilities for further education which were 'adequate' – a level of provision which was never defined or detailed, any more than the FEFC's current legal remit to ensure 'sufficient and adequate facilities for further education' throughout the country. While some local authorities came in the 1970s and 1980s to maintain an expanding FE service which offered wider opportunities for people in their localities, others showed little interest in this branch of their education system. These differences meant that the transformation of the local tech into what Peter Scott (above) called 'a broader community-wide comprehensive college' was uneven across all the areas formerly administered by more than a hundred English and Welsh LEAs. So, instead of a single new FE sector being established in these two formative decades, 'more than a hundred mini-sectors', as Scott said, emerged as a consequence of different levels of political support and varying levels of local expenditure for the colleges. These inherited differentials in funding and the attempt by the new Funding Councils to overcome them are an issue to which we turn in Chapter 2.

The 'transformation' of the colleges and the growth which accompanied it served, however, to create for FE a place in the national education system for the first time. No longer, with the 3.7 million students that the DES recorded in 1991 (2.1 million in colleges and 1.6 million in adult education centres), could they be marginalized by policy-makers. When at last the age participation rate of 16-year-olds in full-time attendance at school or college passed 50 per cent for the first time in 1990, the colleges were teaching about half of all A-level students and so should have been firmly established as alternative centres of sixth-form provision and as stepping-stones to higher education. This had happened in the absence of adequate central state direction. Now the colleges were to discover the implications of being the object of government policy aimed at a second transformation. The price of coming in from the cold would have to be paid.

Chapter 2

1992 and all that

In time all those who can understand realise that nowadays things are being
ordered differently.

William Trevor, *Reading Turgenev*

The 'double whammy'

As we have seen, debate about education invariably precluded FE. Take, for example, the
Conservatives' 1988 'Great Education Reform Bill'. This focused on the schools,
introducing into them a National Curriculum with testing at its 'key stages' and allowing
them to 'opt out' of local authority control, which was also weakened generally by
schools' own financial management. With all this, there was little discussion of post-
school learning, but under the 1988 Act local authorities were also required to submit to
the Department of Education and Science formulae for delegating their funding to
colleges. The constitution of college governing bodies was also reformed by the Act,
requiring at least 50 per cent of their 10 to 20 members to represent local business while
restricting local authority employees, members or nominees to 20 per cent. These
changes thus paralleled the weakening of LEA influence over schools, amongst which
sixth-form colleges were at this time included. They reflected the Conservative view (as
recorded in the memoirs of the Secretary of State for Education at the time, Kenneth
Baker) that both schools, colleges and polytechnics had been 'held back by their local
authority controllers' even though 'they were clearly capable of operating
independently'.

Though the changes with regard to the colleges were at this stage limited, as
compared with those imposed upon schools, the full force of change hit the colleges four
years later. Under the provisions of the 1992 Further and Higher Education Act, a 'double
whammy' – in the words of the Conservatives' 1992 election-winning slogan – was
aimed at FE. First, incorporation – complete independence from LEAs in the new
education and training market. Second, a new funding regime operated by their own
Further Education Funding Council.

This chapter briefly summarizes these two whammies to tease out their effects
upon FE. In addition, we look at far-reaching transformations of the curriculum. These
had already been introduced, but their impact was felt by more teachers and learners in
further education when the sector began to pay the price of coming in from the cold to
join a new order of education and training.

Our summary necessarily condenses a sometimes technical description of complex
change, particularly with relation to funding. We hope our readers will bear with us. The

discussions can sometimes be hard to understand, but they should try to imagine what it was like for the college staff who experienced these changes. Their familiar world of work was reformed in a few short years by changes, the full implications of which are still working themselves out in practice, and whose end cannot be foretold with any certainty.

Going corporate

On 1st April 1993 the further education and sixth-form colleges were 'incorporated'. Under the Further and Higher Education Act of 1992 – the first major legislative recasting of FE since 1944 – they ceased to be part of local education authorities' responsibilities. Instead, newly constituted governing bodies, or 'corporations', became responsible for the assets, the staff and the management of their colleges. Appointed initially by 'search committees' led by Principals, these self-perpetuating college corporations have charitable status. They are, however, empowered not only to provide education and training but to supply goods and services, acquire and dispose of land and property, enter into commercial contracts and to borrow and invest, as long as this is 'incidental' to the provision of further education. The corporations may also include a student representative, although 106 do not. They also have the same right to commercial confidentiality as private companies, although college corporations are not covered by the Companies Act, and can appoint their own staff, setting the framework for pay and conditions without necessary reference to national norms. Their Principals have become Chief Executives working to the new governing bodies which, following the 1992 Act, have few if any, local authority representatives, including instead one nominee from the new employer-run Training and Enterprise Councils.

Colleges receive state money from Funding Councils – one for England, and another for Wales which also covers higher education. The 43 Scottish colleges are still funded from the Scottish Office, though there have been proposals to introduce a Funding Council for them too. Like the Funding Councils for Higher Education, together with the Funding Agency for (opted-out) Schools, the FEFCs are representative of what the Chair of the 1994 Nolan Committee on standards in public life called 'the big quangos', which he numbered at 3,000 with 42,000 appointments to their boards (Radio 4, 16 May 1996). Instead of representatives from local authorities and the other stakeholders previously involved, the Secretary of State for Education appointed 13 large, private company representatives, like the first Chair of the FEFC who was a former Chief Executive of Boots the Chemist. As well as appointing its board members, the DfEE also has powers of 'guidance' and other reserve powers over the FEFC under the 1992 F&HE Act.

Along with the 'Next Step' agencies now controlling most civil services, a spaghetti soup of acronymic 'agencies', 'teams', 'trusts' and 'corporations' have taken over large parts of the local and national state, including the health service, urban development and parts of housing. They make up what Tony Blair, when Opposition leader, called 'the Quango state' rapidly developed by Conservative governments from 1979 to 1996 and which, like Mrs Thatcher before she came into office, he pledged to abolish. These quangos and others now disburse a quarter of all state funding, estimated at £54 billion a year. How much each of them receives to distribute is decided by the central government's Treasury whose power is further increased in this new state.

College corporations are amongst the 'little quangos' that Lord Nolan next went on to investigate. These include the (originally) 82 employer-led Training and Enterprise Councils (plus 22 Local Enterprise Companies in Scotland) which in 1991 were set up as private corporations to channel public funds to training agencies. In the case of college corporations, as independent individual agencies, they enter into contracts with the FEFC and other funding bodies to deliver services agreed in advance. Delivery is guaranteed by the achievement of various specified performance indicators. Responsibility for delivery is thus devolved downwards whilst power – if not overall control – effectively contracts to the centre. The new type of state, exemplified by the new governance of FE, is thus 'contracting' in two senses. As well as contracting with their funding councils, agencies like college corporations can in their turn contract out to other providers of services. Through these administrative and accounting arrangements the rigours of the market have been introduced – in FE as elsewhere – into previously local authority-run public services. The argument for this was that these services would be provided to their customers more cheaply, quickly, efficiently and responsively by a local – and national – state sector imbued not only with the ideology of enterprise but reorganized along the lines of the new, slimmed down, flexible, private sector in place of old and hierarchical bureaucracies.

The piecemeal process by which these new contracting arrangements were introduced is well illustrated by the government's decision to incorporate the colleges. This was clearly connected with the Treasury's need to quickly make up the £2 billion, which was lost through the Poll Tax revolt that helped to bring down Mrs Thatcher. This left her chosen successor, John Major, with the immediate task of finding another way to reduce local government expenditure. There was a precedent in the incorporation of the polytechnics and other colleges of higher education after the 1988 Education Act. Under their own Polytechnics and Colleges Funding Council (the PCFC), these higher education institutions increased the overall funding they received by raising their numbers of students by about a half (from 250,000 to 382,000 in the polytechnics alone), while their unit costs went down by about a quarter between 1989 and 1992. This impressive efficiency gain undoubtedly influenced the government as an example of what could be done with further education. In addition, an elaborate system of funding polytechnic courses at differential but nationally standard rates per student had been developed if not invented by the chief accountant to the PCFC, Roger McClure. He subsequently transferred to the FEFC along with his Chief Executive, Sir William Stubbs, previously of the Inner London Education Authority.

Moreover, further incorporations would also represent another inroad into the LEA's stake or involvement in post-compulsory education, like the local management of schools and colleges also introduced by the 1988 Act (above). In this way incorporation can be seen as the continuation of a long-term strategy to remove state education and training, along with other public services, from local council control. It may also be seen as a further attack upon largely Labour-controlled local democracy, regarded by many of the ruling Conservatives as inefficient if not corrupt. So, while it is true that incorporation of FE would probably have happened anyway, the Poll Tax debacle provided the opportunity to do then what would have been done later. Again, Kenneth Baker's memoirs recall that work had begun before he left the then-DES in 1989 to give the FE colleges the same 'independence' as the polytechnics.

The whole business, however, was rushed through, as a result of the immediate necessity to raise revenue. It was, as was said at the time, a notoriously 'quick fix'. In fact, with the additional uncertainties surrounding the result of the 1992 general election, some colleges and LEAs delayed preparation for incorporation, believing it would never happen because Labour would win the election. In its haste and its own uncertainty over re-election the government surprisingly included the sixth-form colleges in its plans for FE. Sixth-form colleges had always previously been seen as part of the school sector. This sudden inclusion was either a mistake by the then Education Minister Kenneth Clarke, or else it was a deliberate move to make up the balance still required to compensate for the Poll Tax shortfall. Whichever, the result was a chalk and cheese sector in which the future of many sixth-form colleges was for some time even more uncertain than the fate of the rest of the newly independent tertiary and FE colleges with which they now found themselves incorporated on terms of equality and competition.

Needless to say, government rhetoric brushed aside such anomalies. Kenneth Clarke – memorably described by David Triesman, then President of the college lecturers' Union NATFHE, as 'the only man who can swagger sitting down' – focused upon the key role colleges could now play in contributing to the National Education and Training Targets. These NETTs (later randomly mutated to NTETs) were first formalized for the UK by the major private employers' organization, the Confederation of British Industry, at the prompting of the Organisation for Economic Co-operation and Development, a club of the richest industrialized countries. They set ambitious targets for both foundation learning in compulsory schooling and lifetime learning after it. These were expressed as percentages of the workforce (not the population as a whole), and were supposed to reach various levels by target dates. Of course, these Targets had their own quango, a National Council which was responsible for setting and then revising them when they were not achieved. To meet these Targets, an increased number of young people over 16, and of adults, had to participate in education and training at all levels, so raising the proportion of qualified workers. To contribute to this process, White Papers preceding the 1992 Act made much of the need to recognize the colleges and to bring this Cinderella sector, as Clarke called it, into the mainstream of the education system by giving its colleges a new status, new management and by developing their curricula in line with the needs of a modernizing economy.

Behind the government's wider justifications for the reform of further education was an awareness of the relatively poor performance of 16–19 education and training in the UK. There was also a recognition that the previous approach, based on the German model of separate schooling for a minority and Youth Training for a majority, which was tried from 1976 to 1987, had failed to address this problem. These criticisms were detailed in the joint report of the Audit Commission and the Office for Standards in Education, published in December 1993, which contrasted the low age participation rate in continuing education post-16 with other developed countries. For, while there had been a shift to what has been called a 'medium participation' post-compulsory education and training system, the rate of increase slowed and then declined for the first time for ten years from its peak of 72.6 per cent of all 16-year-olds in 1993 to 70.7 per cent by 1995.

(Though the Heads of Careers Services Association recorded the percentage staying on in 1995 at only 67.6 per cent.)

The recommendation of the Audit Commission/OFSTED Report was that steps be taken to ensure that public money was spent more effectively. There was at that time no attempt to collect reliable information on student enrolment and achievement on all FE courses, including 'drop-out' of students from them. The report alleged that typically between 30 and 40 per cent of all FE students failed to successfully complete the course on which they enrolled, so wasting £350 million a year. An even greater proportion failed to complete training courses run by TECs and LECs. In 1992, less than 30 per cent of YTS graduates had acquired a vocational qualification, and most of these were at the lower levels (i.e. at or below GCSE equivalent). Drop-out and failure on academic courses, particularly GCSE retakes but also A-levels, were also high, even in sixth forms.

An early FEFC circular showed that costs varied considerably between colleges – for both academic and vocational students. These ranged from an average per student of £1,486 at Barnfield College in Luton to £5,579 at a typically expensive agricultural college, Kirkley Hall in Northumberland. These figures were, however, disputed by the colleges and others involved for ignoring other sources of funding and taking insufficient account of part-timers and other factors. There were also pronounced variations in class sizes and in the number of hours students were taught on the same courses in different colleges. These in turn bore little relation to student achievements in terms of the qualifications they obtained.

The English Further Education Funding Council which was also established by the 1992 Act therefore took as its aims, as set out in its circular 93/12 of June 1993:

- to secure throughout England sufficient and adequate facilities for further education to meet the needs of students, including those with learning difficulties and/or disabilities, and the communities in which they live;
- to contribute to the development of a world-class work-force as envisaged in the National Education Training Targets;
- to promote improvements in the quality of further education;
- to promote access to further education by people who do not participate in education and training but who could benefit from it;
- to ensure that the potential of the sector and its financial needs are properly represented at national level.

This was not a plan but a statement of indicative aims, though not as specific as the National Targets. As William Stubbs declared, the FEFC was not a planning organization. So, while it can earmark for priority areas, the FEFC presides over a free market system. And, although it has powers to plan, the Council is not obliged to respond to the suggestions it receives from its nine regional committees as to the sufficiency of FE provision in their areas. As a FEFC spokeswoman was quoted as saying in the *Times Educational Supplement* (8 December 1995), 'It is a matter for colleges to decide what they offer and where. It is not for the Council to dictate what they should and should not be offering.' It is the colleges that attempt to plan (see Chapter 6).

The FEFC aimed to meet the criticisms of the previous approach to further education and training, and it was in the light of this critique that the new Council had been established to channel public funding to the colleges. The extent of the culture change which this new form of funding involved cannot be overestimated. The old world tended to be governed by a number of certainties that meant people felt they knew where they were. The new funding regime tore up this secure existence. The Principals became Chief Executives who were responsible for their budgets, the employment of their staff (teaching and support) and for the future of their 'business', the 'business' being the marketing of their courses and the recruitment and successful progress of their customers, the students. This was the new business of learning which the new funding method introduced.

It is in the area of funding that the 1992 Act has had its greatest impact, so that it is not an exaggeration to say that changes in the management, the organization and the student experience of further education have been driven by the changes in funding. For these reasons, it is necessary to explain as briefly and simply as possible the complexities of the new funding method, which the Council based on the experience of the PCFC. Byzantine though the details of this method are agreed to be by all who labour under its constraints, this outline explanation sets out to make plain the differences compared with the old method of funding the colleges.

Funding by numbers

Until 1988, local councils determined the annual budgets for their colleges according to central government policies for local expenditure. The colleges' budgets were determined amidst competing claims from the other local services for which the local councils were accountable to their electorates. This, as we have shown, resulted in very uneven provision of further education nationally. The inheritance from the LEAs led to variations between the colleges that reflected their different financial circumstances and priorities, as well as the varying costs of different areas of FE provision that range from expensive vocational courses in workshops and laboratories to cheaper classroom-based subjects. This situation was not altered by the delegation of budgets to colleges by most LEAs from 1988 to 1992.

The 1992 F&HE Act empowered the Funding Council to introduce, for the first time, a national system and common level of funding for all colleges. The FEFC began this task by consulting college Principals on the new funding method – soon dignified with an '-ology' into 'methodology'. At the same time, the newly independent Principals were assured that, for the first year of incorporation, 1993–94, historical levels of funding inherited from the LEAs would be maintained. Amongst the 70-odd circulars the FEFC issued in its first 18 months, at a rate of at least one a week, the crucial document in this consultation process was 'Funding Learning'. This was sent out in December 1992. It outlined six alternative models of funding for the new sector. These suggested different ways of meeting the government's stated aim of an efficient system of funding common to all colleges, improved management of colleges and higher student participation and achievement.

The only programmes of learning that would be funded would be those listed as approved by the Secretary of State under Schedule Two of the 1992 Further and Higher Education Act. As listed by FEFC Circular 92/09, these were:

(a) Vocational qualification, (b) GCSE or GCE A/S level, (c) access course preparing students for entry to a course of HE, (d) course which prepares students for entry to courses listed in (a) to (c) above, (e) basic literacy in English, (f) teaching English to students where English is not the language spoken at home, (g) basic mathematics, (h) proficiency or literacy in Welsh, (j) independent living and communications skills for those with learning difficulties which prepare them for entry to courses listed in sections (d) to (g).

The payment for these programmes would be numbers-driven. The colleges would gain the extra funding promised by the FEFC in 1992, only if they could attract and retain 25 per cent more students over the next three years.

The funding method adopted was heavily flagged by the FEFC as the preferred option from the alternatives it had proposed. It presented a contrast to the often opaque manner in which local authority decisions had previously been brokered, a process that involved various negotiations between elected councillors, council officers and college Principals. Instead, for the first time, the funding of colleges would follow a national formula that would be applied to all. It was also intended to be easy to understand, transparent to all colleges and fair to all students.

In contrast with the previous situation, when LEAs decided upon college budgets chiefly against a single count of student enrolments in the first term of the preceding year, units of funding are the currency of the new method. Units are earned by colleges as students enrol on programmes of study, remain on them and successfully complete them by achieving their 'learning goal' or qualification. Thus, a student who leaves a programme before completion generates fewer units and less income for the college than one who stays on course and gains full certification for it. The system requires that colleges make five annual 'returns' to the Funding Council to provide evidence of enrolment and then retention of students at three 'census' points in the year and, finally, of student achievement at the conclusion of programmes. There are also extra units to be earned by students with learning difficulties or needing additional support in the core (or 'key') skills of literacy, numeracy and computer skills, as well as for English language-learning, for child-care and for fee remission.

In the new system, variations in the costs of the many courses offered by colleges are reflected in differential levels of funding. Classroom-taught subjects are, for example, rated at a lower tariff (i.e. worth fewer units) than laboratory or workshop-based subjects which use expensive equipment and materials. The FEFC's Tariff Committee has worked on this issue since 1993 and aims to list all 20,000 qualifications recognized for funding with a unit value, regardless of mode of delivery, in the near future.

Each year the FEFC makes a funding agreement or contract with each individual college. The funding agreement consists, first of all, of a main allocation which is a sum paid by the FEFC in return for the college meeting the targets it sets itself for enrolling students and keeping them on course to complete their learning programmes. This main allocation is made up of 90 per cent of the previous year's allocation (the 'core funding' guaranteed to all colleges). To get more than 90 per cent, a college has to bid for additional units. So colleges can maintain or increase their funding from the FEFC only by increasing the number of units that they deliver. As the main allocation reduced year on year – colleges receiving 90 per cent of 90 per cent and so on over five years – the result was that the amount paid per student dropped by an average of 3.5 per cent per annum. The system meant that a college could not stand still and failure to grow would set a college budget on a downward spiral.

On top of the core allocation, the second part of the FEFC's funding allocation is made up of the additional units that a college bids for, that is the growth it reckons it can achieve over the year. The FEFC introduced a further incentive to growth by identifying part of each college's allocation as a Demand Led Element (the DLE), which was not cash limited by the Treasury. Although these units were paid for at a lower rate, colleges could still get more funds than in previous years if they expanded the 'demand-led' funding available for extra students. There is no limit on the amount of additional funding a college can earn through the DLE – though government suddenly threatened to remove it in January 1997 but then reinstated 80 per cent of it until the end of the 1997 teaching year. As well as receiving the standard rate for their main allocation (at present £12.33 per unit) and a flat rate of £16.68 for the DLE (to be reduced to £12.50 in 1997–98), a college also receives £6.50 for every unit it generates (at least until 1998).

This method of funding is the means by which the FEFC hoped to arrive at a national, common level of funding for all courses. In this system, it was intended that the wide inherited divergences in college funding at incorporation be reduced so that within only three years the Average Level of Funding (ALF) of every college would lie within a range of plus or minus ten per cent of the median for all colleges. This target was partly achieved at the end of the three-year period of convergence around a national ALF of £18.50 (to reach £15.75 by 2000). The ALF was obtained by dividing a college's total income from the FEFC by the number of units generated by its students. This policy of 'convergence' caused particular problems for the highly funded colleges – those with high ALFs – as they were required to maintain and develop their services on a level of funding that was being reduced annually. A minority of colleges, which had historically been the lowest funded by their LEAs, gained relatively within an overall net reduction of 3.5 per cent per annum by the procedure. The national target set in 1992 was for a growth of 8.5 per cent a year in student numbers, subsequently reduced to 5.6 per cent.

If an individual college failed to achieve the agreed targets – through under-recruitment or higher than anticipated drop-out, for instance – the Council would 'claw back' the money overpaid in the next financial year. Like the polytechnics and other HE colleges before them, and the universities which now joined them in the competition to recruit more undergraduates and other students, FE would therefore have to do more for more students on less money in order to increase their overall income. (Though on a third less resource per student than the universities and HE colleges, despite the fact that most further and adult students have always paid tuition fees.)

By attaching 'units' of funding to individual students, the new method was intended to encourage participation and retention. This required colleges to create and maintain records for all students in order to provide auditable evidence in support of their claims for funding. Later, a detailed Individual Student Record (the ISR) recorded this data in a way that proved beyond the capacities of most colleges and their computer software to collect and return. Despite extended deadlines, by mid-1996 more than 300 colleges still had to return their 1994–95 funding claims to the FEFC. In January 1996, after he had announced his resignation from the FEFC, William Stubbs actually apologized to colleges for the difficulty that the ISR had caused colleges.

The implications of these acknowledged shortcomings throw in doubt the whole working of the FEFC funding method, since it relies upon the accuracy of the ISR data returned by the colleges. The reliability of unit data has in fact been in doubt ever since the Spring 1994 conversion exercise when colleges first converted their 1993–94 enrolment forecasts into 1994–95 forecast units. A confidential letter dated 26 January 1996 from William Stubbs to Roger Ward, Chief Executive of the Colleges' Employers' Forum, referred to the 'so-called data' upon which the whole funding method relied. If the returns to the FEFC are so unreliable, this means that the entire league table of Average Levels of Funding is based only upon *estimates* made by the colleges in the previous year.

Since 1994, 169 colleges have had their 1993–94 student number returns qualified by auditors, while up to ten colleges had their 1994–95 funding agreements retrospectively changed because the FEFC admitted the defects in college data. Although these errors were known about, they have yet to appear in any FEFC circular, though the FEFC has publicly admitted to errors in its DLE programme. These errors alone can produce variations of up to ten per cent in any individual college's units, which is equivalent to over £2 of its Average Level of Funding, adding up to millions of pounds in many cases.

The fall in college incomes due to convergence was accelerated by the further cuts which followed Chancellor Clarke's 1995 budget. These marked the end of the brief phase of growth from 1993 to 1996 and also cut capital funding from £159 million to £59 million per annum. The Average Level of Funding is therefore falling year on year, though an individual college can never be sure by how much the median convergence point is shifted downwards by the relative costs of all the other colleges. This makes the funding method inherently unpredictable, as well as inherently unreliable – as we have already indicated.

It also became harder for colleges to meet the targets for increased numbers of students if they had already expanded considerably before the new funding was introduced. The knock-on effect was that it became increasingly difficult for all colleges, as new sources of students were mopped up in competition with schools, Modern Apprenticeships and other training schemes, as well as the surviving adult education institutions, universities and other HE institutions. Potential students still remaining outside the system were the hardest to attract and recruitment to the FE sector thus flattened out in 1995–96. Effort increasingly went instead into keeping those who were in college on course for completion.

Some colleges also managed to grow by franchising courses to students in employment, in schools and in community organizations, often certifying competences that such 'students' already possessed by agreement with their employers or the schools and organizations 'teaching' them. Very quickly franchising grew to exceed ten per cent of all the units in England, though it represented well over 50 per cent of units in some colleges. Such franchising was often only a short-term measure, since employees of a company, for instance, could not as 'students' be certified again and again for the same competences – though the ingenuity of colleges in devising new 'courses' for accreditation can never be underestimated. (Also, formerly 'non-vocational' courses were repackaged to fall under Schedule Two of approved vocational courses. Some colleges converted flower-arranging into floristry, for instance.) Colleges that went in for franchising in a big way were often those most successful in reducing their Average Level of Funding and thus appearing most efficient. Via 'distance learning' they also managed to include students far outside their own neighbourhood. At one of the two southern England colleges in our study, for instance, a midlands college was franchising to students from offices in the nearby High Street.

To meet their announced targets for student enrolments, retention and attainment, and to avoid the 'clawback' of having to repay the Funding Council some of the money allocated to them, colleges worked to meet the demands of the new regime. This operated for the first time during 1994–95 and has continued with only minor modifications. The FEFC made it clear from the beginning that the colleges could expect no special treatment if they got into financial difficulties; the rules of the new system would be applied without mercy. As the Director of Finance at the FEFC, Roger McClure, stated, 'No college is sacred' in a market in which there would inevitably be winners and losers and the 'least fit' would go to the wall. The colleges thus waited anxiously to see which would be the first to go into receivership.

The FEFC had promised that the new funding method would be reviewed after three years and at the time of writing the Council has joined the DfEE's consultation for looking at a new system of 'Funding 16–19 Education and Training'. This consultation process is covering school sixth forms and schemes for 1997–98, as proposed in the 1996 'Competitiveness Mark 3' White Paper. (The three-year review, which also took place in 1996, appears to have agreed not to recommend any real change to the funding method because, as expected, none of the parties involved in it seemed able to agree on alterations or replacements for it.)

When the new arrangements were first announced with great fanfare by the government, they were greeted by a certain euphoria by many in FE. Education Minister, Tim Eggar, had told the Association of Principals of Colleges that the colleges were to be 'the great engines of change in the future' (2 July 1991). FE was identified by government as having a crucial position between compulsory school education and higher education and training. Its importance was accentuated in the 'special new emphasis' given it in the 1992 Autumn statement. In December, John Patten addressing the FEFC as Secretary of State for Education saw further education playing 'a key part' in improving Britain's skills base so that 'we now need to focus much more on FE'. In January 1993, Conservative Education Minister, Tim Boswell, greeted the foundation of the Association for Colleges (the AfC) – a new lobbying and support organization of FE Principals and governors, with the assurance that 'the Government has laid the foundations for radical expansion of further education'.

After this fleeting moment of recognition, however, 'the Cinderella sector' was quickly banished from the ball back to the kitchen. The honeymoon was over by summer 1994. As Ruth Gee, then Chief Executive of the AfC, recalled bitterly in the *Times Educational Supplement* in May 1996:

Colleges were promised freedom from control and a light touch from the funding bodies. Instead, the colleges have found themselves subjected to a regulatory regime which demands detailed returns on individual students. Yes, there is institutional autonomy but it functions in what some might call a national strait-jacket.

This resulted, she wrote, in 'a sudden transformation of climate' as 'overnight, competition replaced collaboration'.

In the rush to expand educational opportunities at all levels most colleges (and school sixth forms) recorded a year-on-year increase in enrolments, the majority of college Principals declaring themselves confident of reaching their enrolment targets. Yet FEFC figures show that the FE sector as a whole grew by only six per cent during 1993–94 instead of the 8.5 per cent intended. One college manager surveyed by one of the authors involved in a national study in 1994 also privately admitted that 'Whatever the figures show, there's hardly a college in the country that has reached its targets.'

Meanwhile, a second function of the FEFC is that of assessing the quality of further education by inspection. Again FE colleges, like schools, the former polytechnics and other local authority higher and adult colleges, had been subject to periodic inspection by Her Majesty's Inspectors of education, an august professional body operating independently of the Department for Education under charter from the Crown. HMI were reconstituted by the Conservatives in 1992, by which time their whole-college inspections had in any case become rather rare. The FEFC therefore decided early in its existence to establish its own inspectorate comprising 70 full-time and 600 part-time inspectors, headed by a former Chief HMI, Terry Melia. As with inspections of schools by the new Office for Standards in Education (OFSTED), the aim is to inspect and report on all aspects of colleges' activities every four years. This is also proving too demanding and a system of self-assessment was therefore proposed. This would give colleges responsibility for monitoring their own standards. Inspections would then only occur for low-scoring colleges or curriculum areas within them. These arrangements have been postponed, although similar ones were suggested by the Higher Education Quality Council for its institutions.

By Spring 1996 approximately 200 colleges had been inspected. These visits resulted in reports on which the colleges based their 'action plans' for improvements and in summary reports which covered aspects of management, as well as all curriculum areas in all colleges. All aspects of a college's activity are graded by the inspectors from one (many strengths and few weaknesses) to five (many weaknesses and few strengths). The grades are then taken into account by the Funding Council when deciding on a college's future funding. For example, a curriculum area which received a four or five grade in the inspection will not be allocated additional students, or rather 'units', until it has been reinspected and provided evidence that weaknesses have been corrected.

All this pressure has resulted in a huge turn-over in Principals/Chief Executives since incorporation. Many of the old guard of Principals have left and only one-third of Principals who were in post in 1993 are still in their offices, and the rate of attrition continues. This trend has continued despite Principals having raised their own salaries by an average reported as £7,000 by the *Times Higher Education Supplement* (19 May 1995). However, in addition to such perquisites of the executive lifestyle as chauffeur-driven company cars which some have adopted, a few 'Chief Execs' are now employed, like some university vice-chancellors and head teachers nowadays, on short-term contracts with specific targets to meet as a condition of their renewal.

Colleges embarked upon this new enterprising era from different starting positions and have adapted at different rates to the new conditions. In their struggle to survive they are not restricted to FEFC funding, though this is the bulk of their resource. They have the autonomy to make contracts for their services with other agencies, such as the Higher Education Funding Councils, or with private and public employers, or the TECs and LECs to whom they provide training, or – more importantly for many colleges – to the Social Fund of the European Union (the ESF). However, inquiries by the Association for Colleges reported in 1996 revealed cuts in two successive years in ESF cash for colleges. This was in line with a general squeeze on public sector funding which forced many colleges to look to the private sector for more business.

A few Principals even saw themselves as able to dispense with state funding from the FEFC and 'go private' completely. They were in colleges that, like some schools under local management, had accumulated substantial reserves as a result of the new arrangements. Most were not so sanguine however, for different colleges are differently positioned to benefit from such sources as the European Union or by deals with the private sector through the Private Finance Initiative that was launched by the Conservative government in 1996. For example, in the two colleges which this book goes on to examine in detail, 'Home Counties College' gained 25 per cent of its recurrent funding from other sources than the FEFC, while 'Inner City College' secured only 12 per cent annually from other sources. As in higher education, student fees from individuals paying for themselves – particularly if they come from overseas – can also contribute significantly to college incomes.

To take advantage of the new conditions, new trading companies have been set up by colleges and new specialist staff have been employed – in personnel, for data management and for accounting and financial management. New internal structures of senior management teams and of teaching staff have been introduced and quickly modified in the light of anticipated budget changes. 'Delayering' accompanied 'downsizing' – or, even more euphemistically, 'right-sizing'. *FE Now* (December 1996) estimated a staff loss of 13,000 via the FEFC's Restructuring Fund since 1993, while the *Times Educational Supplement* reported (25 December 1994) that one-tenth of FE staff had been warned they could be made redundant within three months due to budget deficits that colleges had accrued. By the 1996–97 FEFC cash allocations, 151 colleges faced cuts of up to ten per cent with few gaining significantly. Provisional allocations for 1997–98 are even more severe.

The shift from college staff being the employees of the local education authorities to the college corporations meant a change in the arrangements for determining staff pay, conditions of service and other employment issues. These had been embodied on quite advantageous terms for staff in the 1973 'Silver Book' agreement between the LEAs and staff unions. For the first time this represented a codified set of national conditions for all lecturers in all colleges, described by the *Daily Mail* of the day as 'a skivers' charter'. When incorporation came around two employers' organizations were formed to represent the new corporations in their pay negotiations with staff: the Colleges'

Employers' Forum (CEF) for the FE and tertiary colleges and, for the sixth-form colleges, the Sixth Form Colleges' Employers' Forum. The CEF, which was owned by the 355 colleges that joined it, from the start took an aggressive approach to the reform of FE staff terms and conditions of employment. (It eventually merged with the Association for Colleges – see above – to form the Association of British Colleges, though 'British' was quickly dropped due to Scottish objections.)

The main FE teachers' union, the National Association for Teachers in Further and Higher Education, recognized the need for more flexible conditions, but so far has failed to find agreement on what the new 'flexibility' would mean in practice. From one union militant's point of view, flexibility was defined to the authors as 'spinelessness'! For the CEF's 'new model contract' included longer working weeks with more teaching hours and shorter annual holidays. In the recent context, where the colleges as employers are negotiating locally with their staffs, it is difficult to arrive at a clear picture of the latest situation on the ground caused by this impasse. In some colleges agreement has been reached on a version of the CEF contract for all teaching staff. In others, those staff whose pre-incorporation conditions of service are protected by European legislation have refused to sign new contracts and have not received any increase in their pay for the last three years. Overall, approximately one-third of main-grade lecturers are divided from other staff appointed – or re-appointed – on new contracts since 1993.

The bitterness of this divide between staff on old and new contracts, with some colleges eventually sacking those who refused to sign new agreements, is aggravating what would anyway have been a difficult situation. The new corporations already faced pressure on college finances resulting from the new funding method and consequently greater efficiency. Greater value for money means 'more for the same or less'. In many colleges this means fewer taught hours for larger student groups and more teaching hours per week/year for their teachers. In the end, it means redundancies. As a consequence, according to the Central Statistical Office, in 1995 alone more days were lost through industrial action in FE colleges than in any other sector of the economy.

The biggest threat for managers, is going into financial deficit – a situation now facing many colleges. For main-grade lecturers, an increased work load is shared with a growing army of part-timers, rented out from a growing number of independent teacher and lecturer agencies, so that their hours can be reduced or expanded as fluctuating demand dictates and often without any security of employment. For students, many belonging to a generation who are the first in their families to continue in further education, the effects upon their experience are paradoxical and varying. They will be explored, along with those of their teachers and the college management, in the following chapters of this book where they describe their experience in their own words.

First, we have to complete the catalogue of change unleashed upon the colleges. It is not exhausted by description of the consequences of incorporation, the new funding method and the dispute over the change of contracts. For at the same time as all these transformations, a new competence-based curriculum had also been introduced into further education. While this did not affect all lecturers equally and while it built upon changes introduced to many colleges and courses within them previously, argument over it now became entangled with the long-running dispute over new teaching contracts between teachers and managers. We will try to disentangle it.

A new curriculum

Judgement of competence, whereby students demonstrate what they can do rather than being examined on what they can remember, would seem familiar to traditional technical education in the colleges. In trade training, practical tests were often used to assess what trainees had learnt. Such practical demonstrations are more direct than inferring what candidates know from how they write about it, which turns written examinations into a test of literacy more than of knowledge about the subject being examined. They can also let students show everything they have learnt instead of sampling their powers of memory with surprise exam questions.

FE lecturers themselves often did not have any professional teaching qualifications as their expertise too was shown in their mastery of their own trade or craft. Similarly, their students often completed their courses – as art graduates still do partly today – with an end-of-degree show of what they had learnt in a masterwork of some sort, whether it was a specially prepared meal, some elaborate brickwork, fine milling, intricate wiring, careful jointing, or a fashion show.

Nevertheless, there were constant complaints, documented for instance in the few studies of traditional day release (for example, Gleeson *et al.*, 1980), that FE courses, buttressed by the requirements of City and Guilds syllabuses, were 'outdated' and 'irrelevant'. These came both from students and their employers who released them from work so that they could attend college. Often what students gained through staying on the course was beyond what was required for their actual job and qualified them instead to move away from the shop floor and into the office. The quickening pace of technological change added to these criticisms of traditional college fare, which typically lagged behind the latest applications of technology in work.

So, when the idea of systematic competence-based assessment was (re-)introduced into the UK during the 1980s from the USA, it took an ambitious new form in a national framework for vocational qualifications. This is a unique national experiment, for Britain is the first country to have introduced such a competence-based approach. It was built up throughout the 1980s by the Department of Employment in opposition to traditional academic study. The approach is administered by its own quango, the National Council for Vocational Qualifications, which set up in 1986 a five-level framework designed to bring order to the maze of existing vocational qualifications and to make them equivalent to and continuous with academic and professional qualifications. Eventually, as we have seen, National Targets (p. 16) were also set in terms of these levels.

The NCVQ framework was based on an even more ambitious classification of competence previously attempted by its antecedent, the Manpower Services Commission. The MSC had undertaken functional role analysis of all occupations in the economy. It aimed to unify academic and vocational learning in a new education and training system to overcome the difference between mental and manual labour in a flexible and multiskilled workforce. The National Vocational Qualifications, which were intended to assess what workers could do in work, were based on this MSC vision, and they also tied in with the 'Standards Programme'. This allowed Industrial Lead Bodies to specify levels of competence in their various sectors of the economy.

Assessment of these competences proved problematic. The tightly defined language of standards was incomprehensible; one Lead Body organizing NVQs in its industry even needed to employ another set of consultants to translate these definitions into terms that its assessors, assessees and trainers could understand! Also, since NVQs were designed to be assessed at work, it was difficult to simulate working conditions outside the place of work, in a school or college for instance. In addition, it is generally held that NVQs are inappropriate for young people who need a broader foundation than these occupationally-specific qualifications can offer. And many employers remain obstinately uninterested in NVQs – particularly the small to medium enterprises which together provide the mass of employment, while larger employers have pointed out that NVQs tied to current practice in their industries make no preparation for future change.

Moreover, the competence-based assessment of NVQs is very different from traditional, academic methods of examining students. The most radical innovation is that there is no syllabus, as only the performance criteria to be achieved in the test are specified. How students reach the criteria is up to them and if they can already perform satisfactorily they merely have to demonstrate this to an assessor to collect the appropriate unit. If they fail to do this at first, they can practise until they are ready to try again, just like a driving test.

If students can learn by themselves, the teachers' role becomes one of facilitating students' learning but, because of the design of the assessment regime, teachers found they spent all their time assessing. And to assess candidates competently teachers too have to have assessor awards from the trainers' and developers' TDLB (Training and Development Lead Body). These D32 and D33 certificates are also of course competence-based, providing evidence that teachers are competent to assess the competences of their students. Further qualifications (D34, D35 and D36) are needed to assess the assessment competences of the assessors of competence.

Despite all this, increasing numbers of students have registered for assessment in NVQs, although these increases appear to be mostly amongst those over age 19. No national figures exist for the number of NVQs awarded in colleges but most NVQs seem to be in hairdressing, construction and catering, plus business administration. Yet, with the decline in day release, more young people in these areas, as in others, are switching to more broadly based full-time courses, such as BTEC.

Since 1984, the Business and Technician (now Technology) Education Council (which in 1996 merged with the University of London Examinations and Assessment Council to provide both academic and vocational awards) had offered diplomas and certificates with syllabuses including general as well as vocational knowledge and skills. Their approach left room for teachers to include relevant knowledge in the units and modules which, like CSE mode threes in schools, they could design and assess themselves. They were therefore widely accepted in schools and colleges. Yet, just when colleges had become adjusted to BTECs, the major awarding bodies for further education, including BTEC itself, but also the City and Guilds of London Institute and the Royal Society of Arts Examining Board, had to alter their existing courses to meet NCVQ specifications of competence. The examining bodies continued to certificate successful students but these awards were accredited by the NCVQ.

In addition to the reclassification of all existing vocational qualifications into the

NCVQ framework, along with the increasing number of people remaining in or returning to education, a new type of qualification was announced in a 1992 White Paper – General National Vocational Qualifications. GNVQs contained the recognition that full-time students do not have the opportunity to be assessed at the workplace since they are not employees. These programmes, mainly in design, health and social care, and business, thus acknowledged that the 'pure' version of competence-based NVQs, testing only what candidates can do in work, is not applicable to their learning and assessment in college. For the visionaries at NCVQ advocating the application of a competence-based approach to all assessment at any level, GNVQs therefore represented a major compromise. Nevertheless, they were implemented by NCVQ at breakneck speed and, as a result, in schools as in colleges, internal verification systems were found by the FEFC in 1994 to be 'not yet working well for GNVQ programmes and there are variations in assessment practices between and within colleges'.

As their name suggests, GNVQs apply to general areas of employment rather than specific occupational roles, like NVQs. They were intended to raise the status of vocational certification in relation to GCSEs and A-levels by underpinning vocational relevance with general knowledge. To this end, GNVQ3, already renamed 'Advanced GNVQ' in 1993, was renamed again as 'applied A-level' by Dearing's 1996 review of 16–19 qualifications (though this reappellation was quickly dropped, allegedly because of concerns for the distinctiveness of A-levels with which, as an applied version of the same, GNVQ might have become confused). At this level GNVQs are largely based on BTEC's grouped course model of National Diplomas in areas like science, business studies, art and design. The Diploma provided a programme combining general education with vocational studies which, if completed successfully, could lead to either higher education or employment.

Aimed mainly at full-time 16–19-year-old students, GNVQ competences and their performance criteria also contain substantial elements of general education relevant to their subject area of specialization. Teachers assess students' work, which is usually presented in the form of a portfolio, together with external moderation. The general element of GNVQs originally took the form of the 'core skills' of communication, application of number, familiarity with information technology, so-called 'personal and social skills' like teamworking and the also oddly abstracted ability of 'problem-solving', plus foreign language learning intended to be added later. Government later limited this list to make only the first three mandatory.

'Core skills' were renamed 'key skills' by Dearing in 1996. Meanwhile, 'basic skills' of literacy and numeracy have been identified as a major problem area in post-16 education generally, but it is particularly with a large number of students on the GNVQ pathway that the issue emerges as critical. In 1994 the Adult Literacy and Basic Skills Unit (now the Basic Skills Agency) found 42 per cent of students in colleges it surveyed needed help with communications to reach GNVQ2 standard and 60 per cent needed help with numeracy. Lack of core/key and basic skills are widely accepted as a major reason for drop-out and failure at all levels. In response, many schools and colleges have integrated basic and core/key skills teaching with additional support where necessary and the colleges have been helped in this by FEFC funding.

The DfE also began piloting these new vocational courses at level two for pupils aged 14-plus. The trials took place in 300 schools in 1994, as proposed in the 1993 Dearing Review of the National Curriculum which advocated vocational qualifications for 14–16-year-olds not taking the full range of GCSE examinations. They were resisted by many teachers as an extension of separating academic sheep from vocational goats down into comprehensive schools. Paradoxically though, it is possible that the introduction of Intermediate GNVQ2 at 14-plus may have the effect of influencing GCSEs towards more student-centred learning (so far as this is possible under the academic content-centred National Curriculum). Similarly, the influence of GNVQ3s may be 'seeping across' into modularized A-levels, opening the door to a possible 'Scottish solution' of the academic/ vocational divide (see Chapter 6). This allows a combination of academic and vocational, theoretical and practical, arts and sciences in five higher exams, instead of two or three highly subject-specialized and academic A-levels.

Yet in both schools and colleges, teachers and lecturers complained that the GNVQ assessment regime combined teacher assessment, student portfolios, externally-set tests and grading criteria in a complex way that was found to be particularly burdensome. As with NVQs, the new assessment process was highly bureaucratic and time-consuming and its introduction coincided with demands upon lecturers for the voluminous record-keeping and student tracking required for recurrent returns to the FEFC. Now additional recording of performance criteria associated with various elements of competence together with their qualifying range statements, that make up units of competence, with a mandatory core complemented by various options and demonstrating underpinning knowledge, all generated more time-consuming paper and electronic record-keeping.

Then, because of the supposed equivalence of GNVQs with O- and A-level (one GNVQ2 equals four or five GCSEs at grades A to C and one GNVQ3 equals two A-levels, which made it even more difficult to combine the two very different types of course), written tests were inserted at the end of each GNVQ module to introduce 'rigour'. Now a new assessment method is to be introduced into GNVQs, based on a few pieces of centrally determined course work, designed to demonstrate a great deal in one go, while free-standing key skills will also be taught and tested separately by written assignments together with a maths test. The one-resit rule, which the Schools Curriculum and Assessment Authority advised Ministers should be applied to modular A-levels, with candidates forced to settle for the re-sit mark even if it is lower than their first attempt, may also be applied to GNVQs.

For the teachers and lecturers involved, the scope and pace of change expected of them was unprecedented. It would never have been applied to the still sacrosanct A-levels, where proposals for modest changes have been repeatedly stymied, most recently by the government's rejection of the Higginson Report in 1988. There is a widespread feeling amongst all involved that more needs doing to improve the internal and external verification procedures to ensure consistency of standards in assessment (as recommended by Dr Capey's inquiry into GNVQs). More rigorous assessment of GNVQs will cost more however, and we have seen that the new funding method, while it may have generated more income overall, spreads it more thinly.

Colleges can be tempted, therefore, to remain with the numerous other occupational qualifications awarded by BTEC, CGLI, RSA and other bodies that have not yet been converted to the NCVQ framework, though they will be in due course.

Indeed, it has been argued by the educational economist Peter Robinson that, initially at least, the introduction of GNVQs actually hindered attainment of the National Targets for Education and Training since even more students drop out of them than fail the A-levels and BTECs that GNVQs have to some extent replaced in FE and sixth forms. (Robinson incidentally also estimates the total cost of introducing the NCVQ framework as – at 'an absolute minimum estimate' – £119 million. This was before the DfEE committed another £10 million to GNVQs in 1996.)

Also, many 16–19-year-olds who did not get the GCSE grades qualifying them for A-level were taking GNVQs as an alternative route to higher education. So, instead of presenting opportunities for a new sort of vocational qualification or helping to bridge the academic/vocational divide, GNVQs functioned mainly as substitute A-levels for jobless young people with lower school attainments than those doing A-levels. However, even though the CBI called for 40 per cent of the age range to be in HE by the year 2000 (50 per cent in Scotland), the latest policy of 'consolidation' of HE student numbers pegs entry to 30 per cent and this policy is likely to be extended for a further year to 1997–98 with only 'modest expansion' promised thereafter.

But, despite the difficulties and the adverse publicity, the new GNVQ courses were popular with students. GNVQ Intermediate and Advanced courses recruited well in both colleges and schools where they were on offer. They attracted students who wanted to do something relevant and vocational and who were encouraged by the different forms of learning and assessment which these courses involved. The prospect of an alternative route to HE may also have been enticing, though it was illusory in many cases. In 1995 129,000 applicants to HE through the Universities and Colleges Admissions System – 30 per cent of UCAS applicants – failed to gain a place.

GNVQs were introduced in five vocational areas, with another five in development, in a rolling programme from September 1992. The number of students enroling for GNVQ courses – the majority of them at FE colleges – nearly doubled from 81,500 in 1993–94 to 162,800 (one quarter of all 16-year-olds) in 1994–95. Business, leisure and tourism, and health and social care proved to be the most popular, whilst Manufacture recruited fewer students overall. While the majority of GNVQ students are in FE colleges, the majority of centres offering GNVQs are in schools which are more likely to offer Intermediate than Advanced GNVQs save in Business. Whether adding more conventional written examination papers to them from 1996–97, will make them more or less attractive, remains to be seen.

Moreover, Dearing's review of 16–19 qualifications also suggested amalgamating SCAA plus NCVQ to make a new Qualifications and National Curriculum Authority (the QNCA, now QCA). This could effectively leave NVQs with employers and the TECs. For, as long as government retains its commitment to the 'gold standard' of academic A-level, the differences between academic and vocational studies will continue and attempts to bridge the divide between them will not succeed. While the latest changes in learning policy may bring greater clarity and coherence, together with greater consistency in standards of awards made by the main examining bodies, there is a clear intention, expressed by Dearing in all three of his reviews, to re-establish a three-pathway pattern of the most traditional type – gold, silver and bronze; A-level, GNVQ, NVQ to be undertaken in sixth forms, FE and in work or on training respectively.

Dearing's 1996 suggestion of introducing an 'Entry level' qualification below NVQ foundation level 1 will not necessarily attract those who are traditionally 'hardest to reach' to remain in school or go to college. In any case, regions in the south of England and elsewhere, which already have very high levels of participation, do not have much room for further increases in participation rates. Most of any future increase to meet the National Targets will therefore have to come from depressed regions or inner cities with medium and low levels of participation.

As we have noted, it is therefore easier for many colleges to keep students 'in the system' by providing opportunities for progression than it is to encourage new groups of youngsters to enter. At present, many of those entering post-16 education leave after one year so that one in three young people still fail to achieve qualifications at NVQ level two. Only 40 per cent of those participating at age 16 are still there at 18, and many have left without achieving a level three qualification. Progression rates between level two and level three courses have never topped 50 per cent. It will be seen from our interviews with staff that this is a major preoccupation of both teachers and managers in further education today. This is in contrast to 'the old days' before incorporation and all the other changes since 1992 when, arguably, lecturers could afford to adopt a 'Take it or leave it' attitude to their students' attendance.

Despite an overall pattern of enrolment increases in sixth forms and colleges, many lecturers, teachers and their managers are sceptical about being able to sustain them in the future. This is particularly true for the FE colleges. Many of them only managed to meet their targets by franchising and by disproportionately large increases in adult recruitment due to the inclusion of 'vocational' adult education of which colleges are now the main or often sole provider in many LEAs. As Sir William Stubbs, speaking to the 1994 AfC Conference, put it, 'scope overall for significant growth . . . in attracting young school leavers . . . is becoming limited', leaving 'part-time education, for those in and out of work . . . undoubtedly the biggest potential for change'. However, as he cautioned, 'adult students are harder to identify' and are 'more demanding and require higher standards of provision'. In any case, mainly part-time adults will not necessarily compensate FE colleges for any drop in full-time students, although the latest changes to the funding method at least now give equivalent value to full- and part-timers on many courses. Even so, as Stubbs warned, 'one part-time student will inevitably always bring in less money to a college than one full-time student'.

In the new education market, staff respond to the pattern of student demand. This is especially the case under the output-related funding which the FEFC introduced where colleges do not get paid in full until students complete their courses. As long as some funding is tied to payment on completion and qualification, it is not surprising there are persistent allegations of assessment abuse, especially associated with the new vocational qualifications. However, the FEFC Inspectorate recorded in 1994 that, although many colleges did not then have internal verification systems fully in place, 'no evidence' could be found 'of candidates being deliberately certificated as having competencies they did not possess'. Yet press and media continue to allege that this is the case, especially in the privatized training market outside colleges.

With so many demands upon further education in the new competitive market for students, the newly independent colleges are struggling to survive. They are funded in an inherently unpredictable and unreliable manner. They are increasingly threatened by absorption into HE on the one hand, and by association with school failure and relegation to training (as by Dearing), on the other. Their future cannot be predicted or guaranteed. The following chapters of this book record the impact these changes have had upon the managers, teachers and students at two contrasted colleges in the uncertain world further education now faces. But first we must set the scene for the two colleges we shall focus upon.

Two colleges under the hammer

These two colleges represent not only the two main sectors of further education and tertiary college but also illustrate the variety of post-compulsory learning in two very different social and geographic areas of England today.

'Home Counties College' is in a market town with a population of approximately 20,000. The County Council is the main local employer but many people commute daily to London and elsewhere. The town has a higher than average proportion of managerial and professional workers in its population, many of them employed at the nearby university. It was described to us by one of the College staff we interviewed as 'a town obsessed with education'. Nevertheless, there are nearby areas 'with a very bad side to them', as students who lived there said, 'There's a lot of council houses and the crime wave is sky high'. The district's unemployment rate was 11.9 per cent at the time of the College's recent FEFC inspection, which, as the Inspectors commented, 'is high for the region'.

Home Counties College was opened in 1989 on the site of what had been a technical college. The College's tertiary status followed the LEA's decision to close the sixth form of the town's only secondary school thus making the college a main, if not monopoly provider of A-level and other courses for 16–19-year-olds. Two other local schools also closed or forewent their sixth forms. Even though it is located at what geographers call a 'node' upon which road and rail links converge, the tertiary college's location also means that local residents – or their older children – are within travelling distance of other towns where there are both sixth-form and FE colleges. Of the five secondary schools around the town, three are 11–16 natural feeder schools in partnership with the College but only 40 per cent of their applications are to Home Counties College. There are also several private schools in the vicinity.

The present Principal was appointed to manage the transition from technical to tertiary college. The decision to close the technical college and open what was in effect a new institution, had been taken by the LEA after consultation on the options for the future of the college, amongst them one that it should close completely. The tertiary choice, with a £7 million capital investment, was made on the basis that the old tech was not viable and that the new college should be a new development in post-16 education in the area. It symbolized an extension of its provision in the traditional areas of vocational education. In his determination that the new tertiary college would not be the old tech writ large, the new Principal introduced new management structures, following a 'matrix' rather than a departmental structure to integrate the staffs from the school and the tech who had to endure the trauma of reapplying for new jobs, many taking early retirement, although there was only one redundancy.

The vast majority of the College's 1,800 full-time students are 16–19-year-olds, evenly split between academic and vocational courses at foundation, intermediate and advanced levels. The college has also expanded into part-time student provision, to bring the total number of students up to 9,000. This includes the local prison education that the College successfully bid to run classes for, as well as learning support for adults along with local special school graduates, plus foreign-language learning for overseas students for whom residential accommodation is rapidly going up. During the day this variety of mainly young people, milling about the shiny new buildings and the grassy site it shares with the school and local recreation centre, gives the College a bright, open feel that makes it a different world from the older and security-conscious buildings fifty miles away in South London.

In contrast with Home Counties' single site, 'Inner City College' at the time of our interviews was located on four main sites, two in its own borough, the others (now closed) in neighbouring boroughs. Inner City borough houses nearly a quarter of a million people but many of its 22 per cent black and other minority ethnic population live in an area adjacent to the College, which is distinct from the rest of the borough and on the edge of which sit the College's two main buildings, along with its new centre opened in 1996. This is an inner-city area of poverty and high unemployment with vast housing estates including high rise blocks and the highest youth unemployment in the UK outside parts of Northern Ireland. The rest of the borough is more mixed racially and socially with many people commuting to work in central London, the largest employers of borough residents being inner London education authorities, the health service and the local council.

What is now Inner City College was established by the Inner London Education Authority in an amalgamation of three colleges during the 1970s. Its history has been co-written by one of our interviewees under the title of the old College motto *Artifex Semper Auxilio*. What was then called a technical college was London's largest FE college and one of the largest colleges in Europe. At one time it had 500 trainees from British Telecom alone, and 200 from British Gas. It was the only college in the ILEA specializing in all the most capital-intensive areas of construction, catering, engineering and – latterly – computing. However, with the decline of associated local industries – as at Home Counties – some areas of work were closed, such as asphalt technology, some areas of engineering and some specialist catering – bread technology for example. In their place considerable provision in business studies, humanities, special needs and science was built up.

Like Home Counties College, Inner City College experienced considerable change in the years before incorporation. With the break-up of the ILEA, it was transferred to its London borough along with primary, secondary and adult education plus the youth service. The hand-over to the borough was complicated by the planned devolution of its own budget to the College at the same time as the borough tried to protect the schools' budget from central government cuts by reducing its grant to the College by a quarter of a million pounds. As a result 80 jobs were lost through voluntary severance, as has happened to similar numbers every year since, while ILEA Inspectors had recommended the closure of the College to the FEFC in their last report on it. Facing this critical situation, the present Principal was appointed in September 1991. However, unlike most of the other inner London FE colleges, Inner City had only one year of local financial management rather than two because the local authority chose not to devolve in the first year in which they took over. Indeed, it was not even possible for them to disentangle the College budget from the rest of education. So, by the end of 1992 the College was not financially sound; it had declining student numbers and an unstable curriculum base. In addition, the salary budget was very high and there was a huge backlog of work required to maintain the premises. Just before April 1993, accountants Coopers and Lybrand reported that the College was not ready for incorporation, partly because a new reorganized management had not yet replaced the old departmentally organized one. Yet the College recovered to receive a very positive FEFC Inspection for 1994–95.

Nearly two-thirds of Inner City College's 12,000 students are black or other minority ethnic and 90 per cent are aged over 19. The College was thus described to us by one of its senior managers as 'an adult comprehensive school'. 63 per cent of students are part-timers and in the evenings the College is attended by students who are employed during the day, many of them taking academic courses. Like Home Counties College, Inner City College in the evening has a very different character than it has during the day. Only 13 per cent of all students aim for academic qualifications, although an Academic Centre has recently opened.

All this gives substance to the otherwise seemingly obvious slogan that 'Inner City is not Home Counties', even though they are, like all other colleges, supposedly treated fairly and transparently by the new funding method. Yet the business of learning in the two places has many similarities. For a start, both colleges now operate on an Average Level of Funding of around £20. Inner City College managed to reduce its funding level by more than any other inner London college from the third highest funded level in London. Home Counties College also made substantial reductions. Both colleges also claim retention rates for all students of 85 per cent at Home Counties and 75 per cent at Inner City.

The following chapters show how this business of learning is experienced by both staff and students at the two colleges.

Chapter 3

Managing the corporate college

The shifts and turns which seem particular to any one large institution can in
themselves be seen as a model for the wider society in which they live.
Dennis Potter, James MacTaggart memorial lecture, Edinburgh, 1993

Two colleges, two strategies and two styles of management

This chapter focuses on responses to the twin demands of incorporation and the new
system of funding in the two colleges whose circumstances were briefly outlined in
conclusion to the last chapter. As that outline showed, both Home Counties and Inner
City experienced considerable upheaval due to recent local and national changes. Their
Principals – now Chief Executives in the nomenclature of the new age – and their staffs
were then faced with further transformations as they adapted their structures and
procedures to the needs of their new status and the demands of the new Funding Council.

In the first section of this chapter we therefore reflect the views of the Principals of
our two contrasted colleges as they described their experiences and responses. We hope
this gives some sense of their very different approaches, as well as more of a feel for the
two colleges themselves. We then go on to contrast the business of learning in Home
Counties and Inner City by including in the remainder of the chapter the part played by
the rest of the Senior Management Team (SMT) – the core management – in adapting
their colleges to their new contexts and their views on these changes. In subsequent
chapters their perspective can be compared with that of the teachers and then with that of
the students at the two colleges.

Both Principals were clear that, while further education had initially been given a
more prominent role in the education system, the means adopted – independent status and
per capita funding – was likely to lead some colleges to fail. While the Principal at Inner
City acknowledged John Major's personal identification with further education as a means
of raising the skills and qualifications of the British workforce, the resulting situation she
saw as 'Darwinian'. As she said: 'the Tories will take casualties ... the Tories are prepared
to pay the price' of college closures by following their chosen means to this end.

The Principal at Home Counties, also taking a wide perspective, saw the recent
changes in FE as 'just a small part of a very significant social development within UK Ltd
... around the whole question of fundamental ideology ... that of the New Right'. Within
this world-view, the new funding and the new status of the colleges were all part of
changing the culture of UK PLC to compete in the global market. Like the Principal of
Inner City, he acknowledged that there were weaknesses in the old FE which needed to
be addressed but went on to make the point that:

Post-Thatcher we have seen a much bigger onslaught on the public sector . . . [in which] we are seeing a reduction in the state and an increase in private enterprise and [ways in which] private enterprise can be brought in to control previously state enterprises . . . In the new circumstances of quasi-autonomy that we now have of managing ourselves as a business . . . some will flourish and grow and others will wither and die . . . And the clear message of the FEFC to Principals is: 'Yes, it is bloody painful but get on with it and if you can't do it, step aside because there will be someone else who can.'

Threats as much as challenges have therefore been the reality faced by the two colleges and their Principals in the last few years. Different styles of management would respond differently to these challenges/threats. The particular style of leadership the Principal chooses to adopt in response to the specific circumstances in which they find themselves derives from their personality and values. At Inner City, a management style of high visibility was signalled by photographs of the Principal above the mission statement that greeted students all over the College. As a result, all students interviewed knew who the Principal was and attributed all change to her personally. This style of leading from the front was also one of high risk if anything ever went wrong.

By contrast, even though the Home Counties' Principal thought 'There has to be something charismatic about leadership for it to be bought into', none of the students interviewed had met him or were sure who he was. However, one of the teachers we interviewed assured us, 'He's on first name terms certainly with most of the full-time staff . . . and the part-time staff as well.' Such personal relationships were possible in a college with only 159 full-time equivalent teachers, as compared with 487 altogether at Inner City. Perhaps this made a more self-effacing style of management more appropriate, a behind-the-scenes influence that had extended, one of the members of his Senior Management Team told us, 'right down to the placing of the last doorknob' in planning the new buildings for the new tertiary college.

The very different styles of management had at both colleges been successful in meeting the new challenges in terms of expanding student numbers to reduce their colleges' Average Level of Funding. In Inner City, the Principal told us that for a long time under the ILEA.

Local students did not get into this college – local employed students did. Students in Inner City went to Another College . . . [Now] there are more students. They're more local and they are treated with more respect . . . The carpet's in the classrooms. In two years we'll have all the classrooms to corporate standard: whiteboards, blinds, matching tables and chairs. [By comparison] the staffrooms are dreadful. We only just started on them last year . . . The first refurbishment I did was the student canteen. I spent a fortune on it and the staff told me it would be trashed in a month and it's never been trashed . . . I argued this with the governors – two million pounds on computers. This is my retention strategy . . . I don't have a big reception place with receptionists and pretty little ladies in suits. My big guys [security guards] are at the front because that's a very clear message as well about how precious this place is and you don't trash it.

The only thing we don't do in this college is hairdressing . . . We specialize in variety – that's our strength and weakness. [Yet she recognised] The funding method is driving colleges towards discarding the expensive areas of the curriculum which . . . for my community, the community that this college is based in, a vocational curriculum appeals . . . I'm not competing for 16-year-olds. In this location, the curriculum purpose for 16-year-olds is best served in schools.

The College was nevertheless 'making a move in' on school sixth forms, which in the Principal's opinion were too small to survive, by setting up an Academic Centre for GCSEs, A-levels and access to HE (for adults as well as 16–19-year-olds).

The main direction of Inner City College was, as the Principal stated, 'counter-cultural . . . as everybody else flees to dump their construction and engineering, I am bringing in more vocational areas of work'. This was also 'counter-intuitive' for 'The future for us is to go back to where we used to be . . . Everybody wanted us to become a generalist college [but] this college is becoming specialized [building on] the dowry from the borough . . . that we were a specialist college.' From being 'a college that had its arse hanging out of its trousers' when she took over, she was able to write in the College Newsletter three years later: 'We have no problems with drugs or violence and there's no graffiti [with] 11,000 students in one of the country's poorest areas.' So, as she told the 1996 Corporation AGM, Inner City was 'a college that has changed from a largely day-release college towards one that is moving towards higher education', while still maintaining its open-entry to local students and drawing many of them on towards HE without attaching itself as a satellite college to any one university.

For Home Counties Tertiary College such a strategic direction towards higher education was not possible. While it could aim to attract more adults, it could not specialize in technical education. Indeed, the old 'hard vocational' areas of building construction and motor vehicle mechanics had been closed and, while opening up the new 'soft vocationalism' of IT, hair and beauty, media studies, etc., the College was hardly in a position to follow the precedent of the Colleges of Advanced Technology and polytechnics which eventually became universities. Instead, Home Counties' relation to higher education was, at least for half its present full-time students, providing academic preparation for higher education. This role meant that the college would be in competition with local school sixth forms and colleges.

What made the position particularly parlous was the geographical location we have already described. As a result, the Home Counties Principal said:

The vast majority of our students are travelling past the doors of nearer alternative post-16 provision. This college could literally disappear overnight. Now that's a desperate scenario as compared with colleges in large conurbations, which have only got to be there to exist.

Even though, he continued:

This is a successful college – produced a surplus – made my growth – got new contracts . . . We have been able to buffer ourselves over the last three years, how long this could continue was illustrated 'very simply':

> In year one we were able to stash away £530,000 of reserves, last year we stashed away just over £300,000 of reserves and this year we shall stash away about £65,000 of reserves. Now you can see what's happening is that we are absorbing the cost, the extra costs, by reducing our ability to put money aside for contingencies and investments in capital. Now what happens next year? We're on the bottom line now; £65,000 means that there's none. So if we carry on at this funding regime we have got to cut our service, not cut our contingency . . . My mission may have to be rethought. My mission at the moment is very largely based on those old public sector values [of] equity, justice, identifying and seeking to meet the community's needs.
>
> I have just done my analysis for the next three years as to what is going to have to happen to our budget and I know that half a million is going to have to come out of our expenditure over the next three years . . . Now that's substantial – we're on a budget of about eight million . . . It would seem to me as though a lot of colleges are in the same position of having suddenly to react to very adverse financial circumstances, make multiple redundancies, create chaos in their own organizations which actually then creates a further downward spiral.

In the Principal's view this could not go on for much longer and the Funding Council would have to use its statutory powers of direction to channel funds to encourage mergers in the longer term, along with co-operation instead of competition between schools and colleges. 'I have no doubts they will go down that route.'

These questions of the future direction of further education that have been raised by our interviews with the Principals of these two colleges will be considered further in Chapter 6. Meanwhile, the discussion of the business of learning from a management perspective will be taken up by the members of the two colleges' Senior Management Teams.

The governors and the Senior Management Team

The Principals are accountable as Chief Executives to new governing bodies. The general impression from our conversations and observations is that governors at the two colleges have been given, or have taken, a strategically distanced role. Generally, the full corporation only meets on three or four occasions a year, a frequency not likely to involve members in detailed decision-making. On the other hand, since important work is done in sub-committees (e.g. audit, estates, finance and general purposes), there are opportunities for governors with expertise, in accounting and financial management for instance, to contribute to the management of the college through advice and supervision.

Moreover, the governing body could also play a role in 'recreating accountability' in the absence of elected representatives, as the Principal of Inner City suggested. This was achieved, she said, through choosing business governors who 'just happen to be black with the right kind of value systems' and 'we've set up community forums and student forums'. As a result:

I think if I went and Inner City College did an about-turn, the heads of the local schools would complain, community groups would complain . . . and if they caused enough fuss the governing body would have to do something, or somebody would have to do something.

Yet, in the view of some Senior Managers at Home Counties:

It's basically a strategic meeting three times a year, just once a term and, as long as they trust him, the Principal will get on with it.

Nevertheless:

I think the governors appreciate having someone there to actually answer the detailed questions . . . it must be comforting to a governor with all the real responsibilities they've got if things go wrong, to know it's not all resting on one person's shoulders.

So:

They don't say to us, 'We want you to increase by five per cent or ten per cent.' We say to them, 'We think it would be a good idea for us to grow by five or ten per cent because of the following reasons' [and] so far they've usually agreed . . . because they hardly any of them really know very much about what you're doing anyway except in very general terms . . . It's more important that they know us and have got confidence in us as managing the place than that they try to understand.

So far this confidence had been maintained.

This account of the role of governing bodies in the running of college corporations was confirmed by an investigation undertaken at the same time as our own into local public spending bodies that included Inner City and three other colleges, four housing associations and three Training and Enterprise Councils. Although based mainly on the views of board members, unlike our own interviews with the college side of the Corporation, the as yet unpublished report of this research mentions from the governors' perspective, 'The problem of discharging a strategic role when one did not really know what was going on.' It also quotes one governor (not at Inner City, but at another college) to the effect that the old and larger board pre-incorporation 'was much more interventionist', whereas the new Corporate board 'always supported the Principal's position – this is partly due to the loss of independently minded local government representatives and the loss of expertise from LEA officers'. A Chief Executive is also quoted to the effect that he avoided disagreement with his board by 'preparing the ground' before meetings, 'rehearsing' and 'picking off' influential members, using the Chair of the Board to 'tip them the wink'.

The key elements in the day-to-day running of the colleges and the drafting of important documents like the strategic plan are therefore undertaken by the Principal and her or his team of senior staff. Something like the strategic plan would normally also be taken to the Academic Board of a college. This body, which every college must have, comprises both ex-officio and elected staff and student members and functions as a forum for college-wide discussion of matters related to the academic work of the institution with a view to 'advising' the Principal on the standards, planning and development of that work. In general the business of the Academic Board tends to be led by the Principal (who is its Chair) and senior managers, though it can occasionally be an arena in which debate on college priorities and proposed new initiatives can take place. It is usual for Principals to take any major proposal for development to the corporation after obtaining the endorsement of the Academic Board.

The Senior Management Team (SMT) is at both colleges a small and cohesive group of people very different from the old hierarchy of Principal, Deputy and then Heads of Department. Reaching down through the ranks of Principal Lecturers and Senior Lecturers to the ordinary Lecturer, this previous semi-feudal arrangement was often criticized in the past for reproducing 'colleges within a college'. For departments, often with very different cultures, did not find it easy to co-operate and usually saw themselves as in competition for resources. Cohesion as well as competition could occur amongst the various heads of department who tended to be in shifting alliances with each other, alliances that variously excluded or included the Principal, who could also play one rival off against another. Such interdepartmental rivalries could hamper a whole college's chances of survival in a new and uncertain environment.

The so-called 'new managerialism' in FE, therefore, presented itself as a modernizing alternative to these perpetual Wars of the Roses. Moves towards a new structure began even under the old contract when a management spine was introduced in 1991 to embrace the old Principal Lecturers and Heads of Departments. This crucial layer of middle management in colleges then tended to go over to the new contract when it was introduced. (All but two out of about 30 had done this at Inner City as compared with all staff on new contracts at Home Counties.) Their position remains ambiguous however, as we shall see in our interviews with some of them in the teachers' chapter. Behind them, the SMT constituted itself around the crucial figure of the Principal who can no longer play the figurehead role of a feudal monarch but is determinate within the contracting core he or she assembles around him- or herself. This core starts small and then tends to get smaller even as the college grows around it.

How this came about differed in our two colleges. At Home Counties, the matrix structure adopted at the establishment of the tertiary college was modified with incorporation. The matrix was designed to absorb the neighbouring school sixth form and supersede the traditional structure of vocational departments in the technical college. By replacing these with curriculum teams – actually, specialist groups of teachers under a curriculum leader – this tendency to compete was reduced. The necessary co-ordination was now achieved with a more line-managed accountability of the team leaders to one of two Assistant-Principals. Other A-Ps had particular specialist responsibilities such as personnel, quality and finance. Despite this specialization, the Principal circulated all his Assistants with FEFC circulars for the first few years in the belief that everyone needed to know what was being expected of them by the Funding Council, though as one of them told us, 'We've now tended to specialize [as] there's just too many of them to read all of them . . .'

A matrix system spreading the particular responsibilities of the various members of the SMT across the college was appropriate in a relatively small, single-site college serving a large proportion of full-time, 16–19-year-old students. It unified the staff by replacing the old Department Heads from the former technical college and absorbing the school sixth form. The new core management contracted with almost annual restructurings reconstituting the Senior Management Team. As one of them recalled,

> The Principal had to start with a blank bit of paper and he needed a lot of senior managers to see all these new policies through and get them designed and implemented with codes of practice but as senior managers started leaving . . . because by that time things had started to settle . . . so the Principal was quite reasonably able to say 'Well, OK seven can cope, six can cope, five can cope' and I think with me going at the end of this year he was thinking, 'Well, four should be able to cope'.

If expertise in the new functions such as accountancy, marketing and information systems, that had previously been undertaken by the Education Department at County Hall, could not be found within the College, outsiders were brought in to enhance the new importance of the registry, systems management and marketing. A member of staff who had owned their own business was taken on to oversee accounting functions at Home Counties, while Inner City appointed an outsider in this function. Eventually an outside accountant was also employed by Home Counties. This particular member of the Home Counties management team commented that the new system of devolution of responsibilities to the colleges multiplied bureaucracy by recreating many little county halls inside each college.

At Inner City, as has already been mentioned, the arrival of the new Principal saw the departure of all but one of the senior managers then in post. As she related it, 'I met all the managers and said, "You are very welcome to stay but you will have to change" and they chose to leave.' As one of the new team brought in to replace them put it, 'There used to be the barons in charge of the College and the new Principal turned up to sort of smite the barons, most of whom took early retirement.' As a result, the College was without managers for two terms. New senior managers were then appointed in a structure that on paper was not very different from the one it replaced. Heads of Departments became Heads of Schools. These were collected together under four Faculties with integrating functions led by new Director of Faculty posts, only one of whom was home-grown. Together with these Faculty Directors, the SMT at the College forms a core management over the Heads of School who are accountable to it. As a result, the informant above explained, in place of the barons, 'Now it's the princess and the courtiers. I'm a courtier!'

Responsibilities are shared amongst this core of courtiers. The Deputy-Principal, for instance, who was the only other remaining senior figure from the days of the ILEA (apart from the home-grown Faculty Director above), acts as deputy to the Principal and is responsible for the day-to-day running of the College. The Vice-Principal, formerly FE officer with the Inner City LEA, is responsible for strategic planning. Working originally to a Director of Corporate Services is the Registrar whose importance, along with senior managers responsible for marketing, personnel, property and Management Information Systems (MIS) is enhanced. These functions are integrated into the SMT around the inner core of the Principalship. The Principal herself maintains oversight of all these areas and takes care of the College 'in regional and national networks'.

To manage the corporate college effectively, genuine teamwork amongst the core management is necessary to share and delegate responsibilities. While integration amongst the team increases however, there is a danger for them to cut themselves off from other areas of the College. In these instances there may only be indirect contact in the form of the computerized accounts and statistical returns demanded by the FEFC, and from survey responses of their own staffs. Despite efforts to keep in touch, the intensity of their own activity is such that we were told by senior managers at Home Counties, 'I never see a student now. I don't think half the A-Ps do. You know, it's total change. It is running a business from this particular aspect . . . It's much more driven from the centre now because we've got to keep much tighter control than we used to.' This was, his colleague confirmed, 'a very marked change from what I would call a loosely managed structure to a very managerialist type structure'.

While the SMT at both colleges was being reconstituted in different ways, the organization for teachers and students was modified but not transformed. At Inner City, as described above, the inherited structure of Departments was reformed into four Faculties with the constituent Departments reorganized into Schools. In contrast with Home Counties, this recognized the realities of managing a large multi-site, multi-specialism College where there is a need for closely informed leaders of the different vocational areas. It also avoided 'a reorganization too far' at a time when new staff and procedures were being established at an uncertain moment in the College's development. Certainly, the structures and roles of the senior staff differed in the two colleges from what was a modified version of a departmental structure at Inner City to a new matrix model at Home Counties. This reflected the different characters of the two colleges and those of their Principals. Modifications to these different systems, endorsed by the corporation, also illustrate the autonomy of corporate college managements in taking decisions about their internal affairs that would have taken much longer to achieve in the days of LEA control.

This was, as the Inner City Deputy Principal saw it, one of the benefits of incorporation:

> I think the senior managers welcomed incorporation with open arms both as a potential panacea for the financial and planning difficulties that we'd been in and also as a means of giving us the autonomy that would enable us to achieve the things we wanted to achieve educationally, socially and managerially . . . The ability to manage our own budget and the ability to develop our own strategic plan – those perhaps are the two most important things incorporation gave us in terms of management control of our own destiny.

As the Director of the Faculty of Technology, who, as explained, also figured in the SMT at Inner City, put it:

. . . because of incorporation really we're accountable for our own actions as a college and as managers and you sink or swim on the basis of that. And so I welcome that . . . I like the idea of being able to manage our affairs and to develop programmes that we believe are useful to our community and various client groups. [Thus he was able to] . . . restructure my department entirely. I just started with a blank piece of paper. You could never do that under an LEA.

However, the reality of planning was questioned by a member of Home Counties' SMT who said:

we were told that when we became incorporated we would be into long-term planning [but] I don't think we are. I think we're into one-year, maximum three-year, planning and I think the planning is driven around finance and I think it's quite short term . . . I also think we are much more controlled now than we have ever been and I don't mean this flippantly, I actually think we are trying to manage under quite a severe Stalinist regime . . . that's how it feels despite the fact that there's masses and masses of consultation but you know the obvious answer is Option E, so you all fill in Option E.

So, as summarized by the Inner City Registrar:

. . . the management of the college has changed very substantially in that period though at the same time the whole system has been much more centralized and so the college is free but in fact it's in chains because it's required to do what the Funding Council tells it . . . There's an amazingly rationalist, almost totalitarian, model the Funding Council have got about managing the entire system through numbers.

Managing the money

For both – indeed all – colleges, the management of their available finances is the basis of their survival and development at the hands of the FEFC. This section shows how the hand-over from the LEAs took place and the ways in which our two colleges came to terms with the Funding Council's new system.

At Home Counties the change from the LEA was relatively smooth. Relations with the local authority, located in the town, had been good and the new buildings had given the 'new' college a good start with student numbers doubling over three years. Establishing the new systems of financial management and records took about the same three years while simultaneously the senior managers developed their planning procedures. This involved deciding each year the areas in which growth should be 'bid' for and which areas should stand still. These proposed targets would be passed in turn to the Assistant-Principals (Curriculum) and through them to the programme managers. Their discussion would lead to firm targets being decided and forwarded to the Funding Council as the proposed target with the student number targets converted into units. For internal purposes, this became the assumed income for the College, with budgets then being derived for programme areas. These teams could then relate these to their needs –

on the agreed assumption that 60 per cent of income is spent on curriculum delivery (teaching) and 40 per cent on other items like estates, administration and finance. Careful monthly monitoring of spending by each programme area ensures that any request for expenditure which would lead to an overspend – on part-time teacher salaries, for example – is prevented.

This account of Home Counties College's adaptation to the new system, though it enabled the Corporation to set aside more than £800,000 for capital projects and contingencies, does not do justice to the time and effort required to institute new systems capable of recording the key data required by the Funding Council as auditable evidence in support of funding claims. Central in this is the Individual Student Record (ISR), certainly the most important statistical innovation of the FEFC. Funding applications depend on statistical information (which are also measures of college 'efficiency') and the necessary data on each student are very detailed. Basically, the college must record information on the age, agreed learning programme and attendance of all students and these are related to the targets set. This is then translated into units likely to be earned on that programme by each enroled student who continues to attend and is successful on that programme. Registers must be maintained with care and regularly reported to the centre, along with any changes of programme by students which might result in adjustments to the unit.

Let one of the Assistant Principals at Home Counties explain the process in his own words:

> What happens now [is] the planning starts off centrally. The Principal has a session with the senior managers at one of the fortnightly meetings where we agree on the strategy – should we go for growth, should we stay still, are we going to go for part-timers or full-timers, sort of general strategy of what's going to happen next year . . .
>
> So we come to some agreement about that and then it goes off to the curriculum Assistant Principals. There's two of those. They share the half of the curriculum each. They go off and talk to their programme managers saying, 'Look we have got to achieve this eight per cent growth, 12 per cent growth, whatever it is. How are we going to do that?' And so they're all working out how they're going to, you know, where is the best potential for expansion, where have we got space here, where's the market out there, and eventually come up with what they think the curriculum will be next year in terms of student numbers which are then converted into units. That then becomes our income from FEFC. Now parallel to that they are looking at other income, things like international students. That's our bid . . .
>
> So what I then do is to say, 'OK that gives us our income, gross income figure'. You look down and see what else you can't get out of like the short-term staff rates, all that sort of stuff where's there's very little and that really takes, you know, that's 85 per cent of your money gone and you then have various discussions with other A-Ps to find out where there's a real shortage, where was it creaking most last year and see if you can actually find a little bit extra for those parts and bearing in mind that we've got a general understanding that about 60 per cent of our income goes on curriculum delivery and about 40 per cent on all

other things which includes things like staff training, marketing . . . That then gives the curriculum area. I then feed them the figures. I say, 'Look, your staff are going to cost you this much to employ, according to your curriculum plan you're going to need so many hours a week teaching and you've only got this many from your full-time staff so that means you are going to have to employ 500 hours a week in part-timers averaging £19.50 for 34 weeks and that gives them their budget which goes to the curriculum. So that's really how it's all done.

[Even though] It's easy to see units coming with the student rather than units coming with a set of separate courses, the difficulty for a college is that if a student drops out they just disappear so you don't get paid any more for a student that you thought you'd enrolled . . . but in more complex ways if the student drops an A-level, say switches to a GCSE, then you get a change of units because the GCSE is less than the A-level, or a particular A-level may be arts oriented and they were originally science so again there is a change in funding units . . . and all of these kind of sensitive little manoeuvres are happening all the time throughout the two-year FE programme for students and every time they happen the unitization process takes note of them and makes adjustments. So it's, as I say, a very complicated situation and one that's difficult to predict with any great degree of accuracy.

There are so many imponderables because what you don't know is whether some of the part-time students are actually not entrants to the college. They are on another part-time course so you don't actually get entry units for them twice. Once they've entered they have entered for the year. So there's a whole series of complexities underlying that particular area of calculation . . . Another problem is that once students are actually in the establishment you're relying on staff to give information to MIS and very often busy teachers just accept somebody new into their class or lose somebody and have forgotten about them in three weeks time . . . We don't actually do register checks. What we do is to require information from individual teachers about their registers three times a year for our performance indicators, so they know that they're being monitored on absences. In any case, they have to respond to a college questionnaire on how many times have the students been absent for a third of the year and that comes up November, February and May and June as well, so the register is a document which you've actually got to read . . . [but] it's difficult enough to get that message over sufficiently strongly that they fill in the census forms and there's a lot of chasing to be done.

The only thing that we can do is to seek to control as much as we can the unit of funding and that's the whole effort of budget management in a way. It seems to be almost impossible to do.

In the words of another Assistant Principal at the College, all this is 'an enormous and fearsome task' because failure to relate actual unit numbers to the target could result in serious loss of funding through the clawback mechanism explained in Chapter 2 by which the FEFC reclaims money it has already paid if a college falls short of its unit target of enrolments, retention and achievement. The Assistant Principal explained:

Last year . . . the FEFC wrote to us and said, 'We think you've got it wrong; we think you are going to get less units than you said.' And we wrote back and said, 'We don't. This is how we calculated it.' And they were clearly sufficiently reassured that we'd taken a sort of serious and sufficiently detailed look at our expectations that they were prepared to accept our figure.

Inner City College's movement to a stable financial condition was more difficult given the departure of key staff and the appointment of new people in central roles at the time that the local authority was relinquishing control after only two years of responsibility. The Principal told us that during this period she did not have exact figures for the College's annual budget. Once the new Corporation was in place (the Chair, a deputy director of a former-polytechnic with experience of running the finances of a corporate institution) and the new senior team was in post, progress towards control over the finances was made in order to balance income and expenditure.

Managing the curriculum

The impact of the funding method on the essential business of the colleges – the management of the students' learning – has already been considerable and appears likely to continue to be so. We have given some account of the way in which financial factors have influenced staff structures and management styles. In this section we show how the new system leads to colleges taking stock of their curriculum in the sense of the total 'offer' or portfolio of courses available to students. This can lead both to the removal of individual courses, or of whole areas of work, which are seen as no longer sustainable in terms of the income they bring in from the FEFC. It can also lead to the addition of new programmes or areas for which there is an apparent demand. Both colleges have made changes of this kind. In another sense of curriculum management – that of the organization and resourcing of the business of teaching and learning – changes have been made in colleges in the last three years which have significantly altered the learning experience of students and the work of teachers.

In their preparations for incorporation both colleges undertook detailed analysis of their work in all curriculum areas. Reference has already been made to the LEA's closure of the sixth form at Market Town School and the redesignation of Home Counties Technical College as a tertiary college. While this change led to an increase in full-time A-level student numbers relative to students on vocational courses, it did not necessarily affect the continuation of the 'traditional' technical areas (construction, motor vehicle, engineering, travel and tourism, business studies, etc.). As declared in its mission statement, in its new tertiary role after 1989 the College continued to offer a wide range of academic and vocational programmes.

In 1992 when incorporation was confirmed, the College examined its position in its geographical area in relation to other competing schools and colleges. This exercise was undertaken by senior managers for the 'shadow' Corporation in consultation with the whole staff and discussed all areas with regard to the crucial factors of cost and quality as well as market position. The review led to proposals from management to close three areas of vocational work which were not and were not likely to become viable sectors of provision (though one of them was later reprieved). Other neighbouring colleges were competing for limited numbers of students for these courses and the reasons behind the proposal to discontinue them included not only cost but the opportunities for growth in other areas of work which would be opened up in the accommodation released by their closure. After some internal resistance, the proposals were accepted by the Academic Board and the Corporation in June 1992 with some staff in the affected areas being transferred to the receiving college, some internally redeployed and a few took early retirement.

A similar assessment of the course offer was made at Inner City as part of the preparation for incorporation. After discussion and consultation in working groups of teaching and support staff, this resulted in the strategic plan being adopted with the title 'Constructing Capability'. In contrast with Home Counties, this reaffirmed the importance of the vocational curriculum, notably those courses in engineering and construction as well as hotel and catering. This decision reflected the Principal's vision, for which she found backing in the new Corporation. This vision saw a continuing role for vocational courses in the college's working-class neighbourhood, especially if the curriculum was modernized, for instance by the addition of computing and electronics to engineering, or by the relation of electronics to stage and studio lighting.

The Vice-Principal whose responsibilities include up-dating the strategic plan saw this as a 'rebalancing' of the College after the period under ILEA administration when the authority had designated vocational areas to its colleges. Now, like Home Counties, the College was free to close curriculum areas, or to open and expand new ones – new to the College that is. Examples of these latter include art and design, computing and information technology, drama and dance (performing arts). It is in these areas that expansion has taken place since 1993, while the old 'technical' sections have remained fairly steady or declined dramatically. This has resulted in the wide variety and breadth of provision which the Principal views as one of the College's strengths.

There are those at Inner City, including members of the Corporation, who would close engineering courses and use those teaching spaces to expand programmes in what we have called the new 'soft vocationalism' of travel and tourism, leisure and recreation management and other services. At the time of writing, this view has not prevailed and, unlike Home Counties, the broad vocational offer, including the traditional 'hard hat' technical areas, is being retained by Inner City. Staff there – both in the SMT and beyond – deplored the way that the funding method could encourage competition amongst colleges to go for growth in classroom-based subjects that were cheap to provide and where large numbers could be enrolled. This was felt to be distorting college offers and was not what vocationally-related FE should be about. Nor did it answer the needs of the economy, in fact the opposite, encouraging students away from science and technology. As one interviewee at Inner City quipped, 'Curriculum development in FE now consists of scanning the Schedule Two booklet that lists all fundable qualifications looking for the well-funded qualification!'

This kind of discussion about the strategic direction or mission of the two colleges illustrates two aspects of the position in which the colleges now find themselves. The first, clear difference from their former situation is the absence of a local authority with the power to influence the specialist course offer of 'its' FE college(s). The other change is that the FEFC, although it has filled the gap created by the removal of the LEA by channelling public funds to the colleges, is – as it has stated (see p. 17) – not a planning body. This was of course consistent with the market philosophy of the Conservative government that set it up and was designed to increase participation by reinforcing through the funding method colleges' competitive efforts to recruit more students. It could also increase flexibility in response to employers' demands, opening up customized courses as required, though arguably this had always been the case (see Chapter 1).

As the Inner City Deputy Principal said, 'One of the peculiarities of the FEFC system is that although it's centrally based on strategic planning, it doesn't plan across curriculum areas, it only plans in general in numbers of students, any old students studying any old thing . . .' It must be stressed this does not mean that the influence of the FEFC upon the curriculum is restricted to rewarding colleges according to their enrolment of students. In the last chapter we outlined the general principles of the new funding method. In practice the method directs colleges – managers and teachers – not only to aim for certain target enrolment numbers, but also to ensure that as many as possible of these 'stay the course' and gain their qualifications. This, a consequence of finance following units earned by colleges (or by the students enrolling, studying and achieving), has directed colleges to take steps to improve not only course delivery in an attempt to reduce student drop-out and increase success rates, but also to provide pre-entry advice and guidance as well as on-course support to ensure students enrol on courses they can complete. The publication of results, along with word-of-mouth reports of better quality, are also expected to result in increased recruitment in due course.

It is to these aspects of 'curriculum delivery' that college managers have directed their attention. So in both our colleges there now exist frameworks of tutorial support and measures to respond to poor attendance and the difficulties experienced by students which lead to potential absences and departure from courses. While these are not new in further education, it would be fair to say that both within and between colleges the introduction and effectiveness of pastoral systems of tutorial care has been patchy and variable in quality – as compared with the role of class tutors in schools, or the traditional university personal tutor.

Now prospective students (and their parents – if students are young enough to be still influenced by their parents) know that they will have personal tutors who will monitor their progress and that they will have access to student support services for help with financial and other difficulties. This includes a new recognition of the Students' Union by management which we shall see in our interviews with students is given a larger part to play, particularly in contributing to the general ethos and image of the college and the social life of its students. However, we shall also see that teachers we interviewed at both colleges disputed whether the time that tutors and support staff could spend with students had actually increased, as well as questioning how much students in need of support availed themselves of these services.

Another development given impetus by the impact of the new funding method is that of Resource-Based Learning (RBL). Again, this is not new; many colleges, notably some inner London ones, have long had 'workshops' with specialist staff equipped with learning materials for developing students' language, literacy and numeracy skills. In recent years more colleges have joined their library stock and staff with these learning support services to form RBL centres. In such centres at any time during college opening hours students can call upon specialist help and use computing/word-processing stations alongside the complete book stock (lending and reference). Additionally, there are materials relating to the content and assessment of modules in study programmes. These can normally be used only in the centre, but may also be accessed by distance learning. At Inner City the Resource-Based Learning Centre, which cost £1 million, has been operational for one year; a similar centre at Home Counties opened in September 1996.

Again, while there were moves to what was usually termed 'open' or 'flexible' learning during the 1980s, the pressure to free the space and fully equip a RBL is clearly traceable to the funding method and the consequent moves to drive down costs (ALFs). In the college budget the largest single item is the salary bill for teachers (typically 70 per cent of the total). If the teaching hours to be spent with a group of students can be reduced without any harmful effect on the students' learning, then their teacher can be released to take more groups in the week – a clear saving in terms of teacher time and salary. The reduction in contact time with groups – typically down from seven or eight, to six hours a week per subject for the one-year A-level students, and to four and a half hours a week per subject for two-year students – is criticized bitterly by teachers who, as we shall see in their chapter, stress the value of time spent with students, individually and in groups. Yet, in HE as in FE, managers emphasize that when students learn for themselves results are not worse and may even improve (as they did in the former polytechnics where students were arguably 'overtaught' in comparison with the old universities).

In Home Counties the new Resource-Based Learning Centre developed from the 'open learning workshop' which was designed to make modularized units of learning accessible to adults who may not always be able to attend scheduled classes. In many ways this drew on the Open University model of learning. The 'workshop' then grew slowly, along with elements of courses that were simultaneously being developed and tried out; for example, GNVQs in information technology and business studies. GCSE maths was 'taught' entirely through RBL for the first time in the 1995–96 college year. This is an example of the gradual introduction of this approach to learning and teaching, the reason being the cost in terms of the time taken to prepare materials and a desire to take staff willingly along with the development, rather than 'to create chaos and darkness and have to live with that for years', as one Assistant Principal put it. She considered that the educational reasons for the change – flexible access to quality learning materials – were more important than the imperatives of the FEFC funding regime.

Perhaps this would be better expressed as a lucky coincidence. For, potentially at least, flexible learning materials enable better practice to be generalized so giving students both a new and active relationship to their learning as well as a better service for the income they bring in to the college. This was, however, one of the issues over which management and teaching staff views differed most profoundly for it involves a change in role from teacher to 'facilitator', as is often said, and for students from 'passive' to 'active learning'. We return to a consideration of it in connection with our discussion of the quality of FE in our concluding chapter. First, we have to recount in our next chapter the teachers' view of the reality of the situation on the ground and then to look at the students' experience of the business of learning.

Managing the staff

A final area of responsibility for college managers – and the one which has been the source of most conflict – is that of teaching and support staff. The new responsibilities of the corporations as the employers of all staff, coupled with the impact of the funding method, have meant that the staffing of the college – its internal organization, the numbers of different kinds of staff and the terms and conditions on which they are employed – quickly became an issue. After all, as we have noted, wages and salaries make up the bulk of a college's expenditure. This meant that early in the period of incorporation, if not before, the question of the payment, duties and organization of staff within the college would be closely scrutinized, not on a once-and-for-all basis but repeatedly. At Home Counties the process began in 1989 with the inception of the tertiary college, as summarized above. At Inner City it began at the time of incorporation, accelerated by the departure through early retirement of many senior staff.

In the late 1980s both colleges, along with the majority of FE institutions in the country, still had internal structures based on specialized departments. The department was the key unit of identity and organization, with courses, staff, teaching areas and students 'belonging' to it. The Head of Department controlled these resources in what was a separate unit, often without reference to any agreed college policy, especially when isolated from other departments on split sites. Many departments, for instance the old Department of Engineering at Inner City with nearly 300 teaching staff in its glory days (now reduced to 36 full-time), were as large as some small colleges and bigger than many secondary schools.

While this departmental structure was assumed, if not determined, by the national agreements then in operation on pay and grading of staff, it came under pressure as resources were increasingly squeezed. The status and pay of senior staff (Heads of Departments and their Deputies) depended on annual recruitment to courses. If external changes meant that recruitment was falling – in engineering, for instance – this meant that resources (staff, rooms and equipment) were under-used. Meanwhile, in another section of the College there were problems accommodating student groups on courses that were expanding. The rivalries and competition between departments resulted in the on-going feudal warfare we have described. At another level this form of organization led to duplication and inefficiency since it assumed that all Heads of Department had an interest in and aptitude for all the tasks of running their departments – staff management, financial control, course development, marketing, etc. Where this was not the case, departments suffered from failings in vital areas of management and leadership.

New managerialism offered an alternative to the old pyramid of departmental bureaucracy – not only in further education but across all of the public services as new corporate models of 'flattened hierarchies' were imported from the private sector in the 1980s. Whilst they were 'flattened' by the removal of some tiers in the old pyramid of management ('delayering', as it was known), it is important to appreciate that the new structures were not non-hierarchical, as was sometimes asserted. For the new approach to management claimed to modify internal structures in ways that would exploit individuals' strengths in management to create a more professional corps of specialist senior managers in support of the principal or chief executive. The many steps in the chain of command from the apex of the pyramid to its base were thus replaced by fewer but bigger steps. This tends, as we have already recorded, to cut the new management core off from their workforce (and see further below). From the individual employee's point of view, as we shall hear from some of the teachers we interviewed, the new organization foreshortens their career prospects, leaving some of them with the feeling that they have nowhere to go.

In further education new management usually takes the form of a matrix structure in which power over resources is separated from the academic leadership with which it was united in the old departmental hierarchy. Responsibility for functions such as recruitment and marketing, quality and personnel, finance and data management can be given to experts in those areas. They can be imported into the college from elsewhere if not home-grown and examples of both have been given at our two colleges above. These people are included in or accountable to the senior management team to carry out such central, college-wide functions, many of which were previously undertaken for the college by the local authority.

Along the second axis of the matrix are groups of teachers arranged in specialist teams, for example: computing, modern languages, mathematics, motor vehicle engineering, etc. Typically, these have subject or curriculum team leaders who work to whichever of the SMT have responsibility for the relevant issues of staffing, recruitment and curriculum development, etc. Supposedly without heavy administrative duties, these team leaders are empowered to concentrate on the quality of teaching and learning of the students in their specialist area. Similarly, their teams of individual classroom, workshop and laboratory teachers are each given devolved responsibility to administer their own classes and courses. Accommodation is pooled and appointments can be made in response to student demand for particular curriculum areas, rather than as replacements for resignations to maintain the old organization.

We have seen how such a matrix was introduced at Home Counties when it went tertiary and such a structure is typical of small FE colleges. The focus is on the offer of courses by the college rather than by the departments within it and important resource decisions are made and implemented centrally. As we have argued, in a larger college like Inner City it is more difficult to introduce a matrix form and there are practical reasons for retaining the old departments even if renamed as schools and arranged in four new faculties. A modified departmental structure of the type we have described was therefore the most that could be achieved. Nevertheless, the departure of the old departmental barons following the arrival of the new Principal was a clear signal that the old order was at an end. So too was the formation of four faculties integrating the schools beneath them. The schools were not merely departments recreated. They had been, as the Deputy Principal said, 'reduced in number and rationalized, [to] thin out the structure'. The heads of the new schools who were then appointed are middle managers with curricular responsibilities similar to those of the curriculum leaders at Home Counties but with additional other duties. At the same time, the faculty directors have strategic resource and planning responsibilities which they implement as members of the SMT.

The number of levels in the hierarchy of management has not actually been reduced at Inner City College as Heads of Department became Directors of Faculty, Principal Lecturers became Heads of School, Senior Lecturers became Programme Area

Leaders and Lecturers remained lecturers. The regrouping of nine Departments into four Faculties, recreates the departments as schools but without the control over resources that now rests with the Directors of Faculty in the SMT. This shows that at both colleges the effect of the organizational changes has been towards a structure in which senior managers control critical decisions of finance, curriculum and staffing, while middle managers are charged with the teaching and running of courses at the next level down.

The imperative of expansion in competition with rival providers at the same time as making efficiency savings to deliver more for less, both dictated and reinforced by the funding method, has led Principals and their SMTs to centralize control over key functions. At the same time, some responsibility is devolved to subject or curriculum/ programme leaders for the administration and evaluation of teaching programmes. At Home Counties this took the form of a matrix, while at Inner City the relation of Programme Area Leaders (PALs), as they were called there, is mediated through their Heads of School. This in turn places these middle managers in the testing position of managing the teachers through the changes required by the college and also by outside bodies, like exam boards, the NCVQ, or TECs, in terms of the delivery of new courses to more students, increasing class sizes and reducing teaching time.

The effect of all this has been to sharpen the divide between teachers and managers which is examined from the teachers' perspective in the next chapter. An important and contentious aspect of the divide has been the introduction of the new contracts of employment in further education. This real change for teaching staffs followed upon incorporation in 1993. As we will see, it is one of the main bones of complaint made to us by teachers at both colleges, even those who had signed the new contract.

For the time being, it is important to appreciate that a consequence of the new 'flattened hierarchy' was that the contracting core of the SMT tended towards managing indirectly, via the intermediaries of the team leaders, the staff for whom they had various cross-college responsibilities according to the matrix. The tendency which we have already noted for, as one manager confirmed, 'the statistics to become much more important because our funding depends on them' accentuated moves towards management by objectives, setting all staff collective and individual targets to meet quantifiable performance indicators. New technology potentiated this trend. Just as they saw less of students, senior managers were in infrequent contact with shopfloor staff. SMT members at both colleges mentioned to us the time that they spent in meetings, usually amongst themselves. This was despite consequent efforts senior management made at both colleges to 'get out and about' and 'meet people', including attending special occasions such as college forums and 'away-days'.

It is possible that previously – in what everyone referred to as 'the old days', pre-incorporation – contacts between the top and the bottom of the old hierarchy were just as or even less frequent. The difference was that the steps in the chain were all face-to-face relations, so that messages could be relayed down the chain from one person to another, doubtless often with a 'Chinese whisper' effect. Face-to-face contact between managers and managed was only possible now through new systems of staff appraisal that linked all staff in the flattened organization to their immediate line manager above and/or below them in counselling sessions that, while they were intensive, were also infrequent. (They are also problematic for the SMT in a matrix because senior managers then deal with individual lecturers through the intermediary of the curriculum leaders whose team they are in. This puts the focus on the particular area of their concern and not with the individual's all-round performance.) So the SMT attempted to compensate for the new division by using new technology to print out and e-mail messages to all staff concerning the particular areas of their responsibility in the matrix. This leads to what has been called 'management by memo' and was another complaint made to us by teachers.

The SMT members were sensitive to such complaints. They appreciated, as one said:

> There are an awful lot of staff here who are untouched by everything I'm talking to you about. They have [a] different reality and the reality would be their terms and conditions of service, no pay rise for three years, huge new burdens that are represented by GNVQ, our own quality assurance systems and everything else. More students to teach, larger class sizes . . . at the same time some of them will certainly have views that they shouldn't be teaching the students they have to teach, not what they came in to it for, you know – a whole array of things.

And at the other college:

> I suspect that they just think that life is just that much worse than ever it used to be. I really think that. We've got quite a good morale in the staff here but relatively for the FE sector as a whole I think it's pretty bloody dreadful.

Others in the SMT felt that too many changes had been introduced too quickly, for example:

> I have political difficulties with a lot of the things that we've been involved in because I don't think there has been time to evaluate whether they are right for the sector in terms of is it going to enable the sector to improve what it offers to students and I just don't think there's been the time to evaluate that properly.

However, the interviewee added, 'I do think the shift towards a more accountable sector is right and I think that's proper and I think there's a lot of things that's gone on in that context which I think have been models of good practice.'

> As an instance of this she mentioned the state of affairs in the college at her arrival:

> I inherited a department that had never ever been managed. They had no concept of management. People didn't have timetables. People didn't have any notion of accountability at all. People used to cancel classes. They used to swap classes. They used to sub-contract classes. I mean, it was just I felt like I'd hit another planet to be honest. So things that I took for granted, i.e. you had a timetable, on your timetable was put your related duty times, that you knew that you needed to be on the premises for that and if you weren't going to be on the premises you sought permission. I just took all that as part of work life.

It had taken a long process of reorganization to put the new management systems in place. These systems brought with them a new level of corporate control over teachers who were now dedicated to the mission of the college as a whole, rather than attached to their former departments and their own individual ends and those of 'their' students within them. Management had been aided in this task by the realization amongst teachers of the parlousness of the situation at both colleges. It was either sink or swim. The strong lead given by the SMT could therefore win teacher support, even if only grudgingly given in some cases.

As a result, from the SMT perspective:

> I think that most of them think they work in a successful college. I think that is much better for them in terms of how they feel about it all than working in the place as it used to be where you couldn't even see where it was going . . .

While again at the other college:

> I'm not saying, you know, all teachers in FE were bad before because I don't think they were. I don't think you could survive in FE if you didn't care about the people that you were teaching. I just think the focus is sharper and I think people are more rigorous about what they give to young people and adults these days and I think historically people did rush in without really having thought about their class. I think there's a lot, lot less of that.

Her colleague in the SMT added:

> I take my hat off to the FEFC in terms of what they have done picking up on the inefficiencies of the system . . . [because] FE – and I suspect HE as well – was a mishmash of brilliance on the one hand and absolutely diabolical practice on the other.

The new corporate management of the college, together with the new funding method, had enabled SMTs in their own estimation to build on good and eliminate bad practice. As one summarized:

> I think that we have been able to manage the college in an effective way. We have produced a sound budget with a modest surplus. We have reduced our Average Level of Funding and that's been done without any significant damage to the curriculum offer . . . But it's important . . . to adopt a value-added approach to that and to take people from very low levels of attainment up onto the levels of progression through the education system. So to do that we needed to establish extremely good pre-entry guidance and support and counselling. Very good entry curriculum advice and placement and extremely strong support systems for the learning process through tutorials, what the FEFC calls additional support and other means of helping students to learn. And of course the funding methodology enables colleges to do that by ensuring that at least eight per cent of their funding is spent on pre-entry matters and in funding additional support and the other things that you're familiar with, so it was in a sense just the thing that we wanted and I hope that we've been able to take advantage of that in the last two or three years.

This had not been without cost however, including to themselves, working throughout the summer holidays for instance. Let us conclude with two different voices that show this clearly:

> I found it very emotionally draining the first few years. And then we went through that again with incorporation. I think there's a lot of people in the system who are very drained and exhausted by it and I would include myself in that category of person. It feels like it's unrelenting, unforgiving and unacknowledged and that's actually a very difficult climate to work in. Having said that, I think the achievements over the last three years have been enormous. And I think what would be quite nice is if there was some time just to celebrate that so you could actually feel good about being so exhausted about it!

> From the point of view of the service being offered from here it's better. There's no doubt at all everything has been tightened up. We're getting quality. Everybody's looking at exam results and whether people get jobs. It's really being followed through and that's good. But in terms of personally it's a bloody sight worse. I mean, it gets more and more frenetic week by week. You think they can't keep on at this pace [but] it does and it goes faster, you know. I'm quite looking forward to the end of this year [when he retired] I don't mind telling you. I mean, I'm enjoying the job I've got but it is very very stressful all the time.

These perceptions of improvements but at personal cost led to what another interviewee referred to as

> the schizophrenic manager [who] gets carried along on two tracks. The one track is that I'm an educationalist and I believe in all these things and the other is we've got to survive so I have to understand this funding methodology and somewhere these two parallel tracks have to come together.

Above all, from the senior management and Principal's perspective:

> The thing that permeates right through everything that is the over-riding new influence is that you've got to find your own salvation. There was always that sort of feeling, well, County Hall will pay if things really go wrong but now we know that's not the case, so life is that much more stressful. There's no doubt at all about that, a lot more stressful. But on the other hand, the managers are aware that we've got to solve our problems. Nobody else is going to do it for us.

The next chapter goes on to look at how the teachers at the two colleges reacted to the management methods used to tackle the problems or 'challenges' associated with incorporation.

Chapter 4

The teachers' world

Everyman, that has ever undertaken to instruct others, can tell what slow advances he has been able to make, and how much patience it requires to recall vagrant attention, to stimulate sluggish indifference and to rectify absurd misapprehension.

Dr Johnson

In the middle of the matrix

This chapter reveals the impact that the changes, described by the Principals and their Senior Management Team in the preceding chapter, had upon the teachers we interviewed in the two colleges. Our selection of teaching staff was necessarily limited. It does, however, relate to our selection of students for interview in the manner that will be described in the next chapter. We targeted the 14 lecturers who taught our groups of students on classroom, laboratory and workshop 'pathways' at the different 'levels' of Foundation, Intermediate and Advanced. They were interviewed by one of the authors who then also talked to these teachers' line managers (curriculum team leaders or programme managers as they were called at Home Counties, Heads of School at Inner City). Of course, the students' teacher could also be a programme manager or HoS, since – unlike the SMT – these middle managers taught as well as managed. Their teaching load was reduced, so middle managers usually taught for seven to eight hours a week, as compared with the up to 25 contact hours expected of ordinary lecturers under the new contract. We thus worked up – if not chronologically – from classroom/shopfloor/ laboratory lecturer to the Senior Management Team with which we began our account in Chapter 3. This gave us a total of 17 teaching staff interviewed altogether, slightly less than our target but representative nevertheless in terms of position in the organization and of age and experience of the full-time teachers at the two colleges. The elected officers of the NATFHE branches at both colleges were also interviewed.

We begin by retailing the views of the immediate line managers responsible for the shopfloor teachers who make up the majority of our sample of staff. This is because these middle managers are the link between the core Senior Management Team and the rest of the staff. Nearly all of them at Inner City and all at Home Counties were, like the SMT, on a different management salary scale, or 'spine', from the ordinary lecturers. These people are a crucial link in the day-to-day running of the college, dealing both with teachers and students by supporting the tutors in their programme/curriculum areas or Schools to maintain students' attendance, discipline and punctuality, as well as ensuring the delivery of courses by lecturers for whom they may have to arrange cover at short notice if they are absent. They thus organize timetables and book rooms, etc. They also employ part-time staff, organize the provision of technical support, including non-teaching staff, as well as the supply and repair of equipment and other consumables. Most importantly, as we have seen from the SMT's point of view, these middle managers have to be relied on to make sure that frontline staff keep the records and provide the data to central Management Information Services (MIS) so that the college can claim the vital units of funding from FEFC upon which the financial viability of the whole corporate enterprise now depends.

For all this activity, said one, 'Programme is the wrong word actually. They are basically mini-departments.' There are, however, major and important differences between the old mega-departments and these mini-ones. As we have recalled, the traditional Heads of Department in colleges were charged with responsibilities for course development and innovation, the recruitment of students and the management of resources, especially accommodation and equipment but also the running of 'their' staff. This gave them considerable powers and could put them in control of institutions within institutions. In the new incorporated college it is not possible to allow power over resources to be devolved in this way. Decisions over recruitment and allocation of resources to programme areas/Schools are now made by the Senior Management Team to be implemented by the middle managers.

In addition, even in a matrix, as at Home Counties, there are too many cross-college functions to be held in the hands of the contracting core of SMT. So, as a Home Counties programme manager explained, 'You know, we'll have people that specialize in curriculum, people who specialize in marketing, people who specialize in finance. We've got programme managers, like myself – 20-odd programme managers – to deal with all aspects of the College's activity.' For example, another interviewee at Home Counties managed the A-levels programme, the electives programme and the enhancement programme at his college. 'So I have three other strings on the bow as well but to what extent I manage those and to what extent I oversee them is debatable.' As a result of all these administrative duties, as an Inner City Head of School told us, 'over the last five or six years my role has changed from being a teacher and doing some management to being a manager and doing some teaching . . .'

We have seen from the SMT that these middle managers were not involved in the strategic decisions, approved by academic board and governors, of setting the targets for student enrolment and retention made for funding units to the FEFC. However, they were allocated some budgetary responsibility for implementing the consequences of these decisions. They also join in senior management meetings at which the implications for their various curriculum areas of the agreed targets contained in the college's strategic plan are spelt out and they then have to gain the agreement of the teachers in their areas to meet these targets.

Middle managers thus inhabit two different worlds, returning from board room to staff room to communicate the details of the decisions that have been taken by the Principal, even though he or she may also address staff directly in staff meetings or via internal written communications. To fulfil this mediating role, middle managers may have to modify and adapt the language (and the view of reality contained in it) of the Principals and their SMTs to meet that of the teachers who may or may not accept it. For, within the context of an overall reduction in the unit of resource, any change entails teachers doing more of what they are already doing and/or undertaking new activities in addition to their present workloads. As in the case of any intermediary management therefore, the position of the middle managers is an interesting and revealing one. With their loyalties and their functions divided between managing and teaching, they feel ambivalent and they are ambiguous.

This was appreciated from both sides of the divide. From the point of view of SMT:

> I think what happened was almost overnight there was the concept of 'THE MANAGER' – in block [capital] letters – and people trying to grow into roles that they did not understand. And I don't think they did understand them. And [there was] a kind of a lot of anxiety about – What is a manager? How do I become one? How do I change my status from being a peer to being a manager? And certainly I think that manifests itself more acutely at a middle management level than it did at senior management level here because I think senior managers had already largely made that transition. I don't mean status in the sense of importance there. I mean status in the sense of other people perceiving that this is a manager, that this is what a manager is and this is what it means. And I think there's been lots of confusions about what a manager is and I think we've had the whole range of behaviours. I think we've had bullying behaviour – a manager is a bully. I think we've had managers at the other extreme who've felt they're still mates with their mates and that they can manage by being matey and they have found it very difficult when in actual fact they've found that that doesn't work either. So I think we've gone through, you know, quite a period of time while people have understood what those roles mean.

On the other side, from the point of view of one of the union representatives, the divide was very clear: 'Either you are a teacher or you are a manager.' According to this definition, a teacher did not manage in the ultimate sense of having the power to hire and fire staff and a manager did not teach. Yet the apparent clarity of this distinction did not apply to middle managers who, we have already noted, had a reduced teaching load but did not have the power to appoint and dismiss staff, though they might take part in interview and appeals panels and could employ some temporary and part-time staff. Their main function was getting other people to do things that had been decided upon by another lot of people. So, as the Union representative continued:

> There's that layer of people – about 30-plus – who are a crucial management layer in the college now and with the exception of two people all of them are on a new contract. Only about half of them are in NATFHE and outsiders have been brought in and many of them have what I call the new ethos, the new set of values. They use this language of the market all the time and so on. So that is the level at which the ordinary rank and file teacher experiences the management.

Clearly, this interviewee did not share 'the language of the market' and its 'new ethos' and was adamant he never would.

Yet in the view of one of the Assistant Principals at his college other teachers there were coming to accept 'the new set of values':

There is a kind of very funny communication which goes on just below that Head of School level . . . [but] we're doing some programme area leaders training this year. They don't know much. They don't understand why things happen. They're beginning to and the change – I was just talking to a Head of School on Monday – the change in those people just because they get the hang of what the funding methodology was about, they get the point. They see the point and so I think it's going down a level each year. That seems to be how it's going down in terms of getting people, I won't say morally involved with the enterprise that is called Inner City College, but at least being able to live with it whatever their ideological viewpoints or whatever.

At Home Counties the staff as a whole had already endorsed management to the extent of going over en masse to the new contract. Divergences of view remained marked at both colleges however, both within the teaching body and amongst middle managers. In part these depended upon age and experience. New and younger staff usually, but not in all cases, accepted the situation they had arrived into. Their acknowledgement of the new realities also depended upon their teaching specialism. As we shall see, in traditional and declining areas of the curriculum, both academic and vocational, teachers' positions were more entrenched. This was in contrast with growing areas of the curriculum, including new and innovative programmes that had benefited from additional funding to expand with new students, resources and equipment.

Correspondingly, the middle managers at both colleges covered a broad spectrum ranging from those who supported and saw themselves as part of SMT to those at the opposite pole who identified with the teachers for whom they were responsible. For example, one curriculum programme manager agreed with the vision of the A-P above that:

The changes are filtering down from the top with varying degrees of speed. To a certain extent I think that the people at programme manager level cushion or filter out a lot of the changes [for the people] below so that for a lot of people working at the whiteboard face the changes have been fairly limited . . . There are still people who are not aware of some of the implications of the changes but it's slowly happening and things like the change from worrying about student numbers to worrying about units . . . that kind of change is slowly filtering down, so things like the messages about retention, the messages about pass rates, the messages about league tables are all coming through. People are slowly and progressively becoming more aware of their own responsibilities within the framework but it's not total yet and there are still some people I would guess who are all working much in the same way that they did three or four years ago without much change.

On the whole he welcomed the new dispensation, 'in the sense that you perhaps restrain the old kind of maverick departmental barons who used to be in FE, people who go off in their own direction in their own department', but, he added, 'You also make things in a way less flexible, less able to respond on a human level. It's a strange dichotomy isn't it?'

His colleague at the same college shared no such sense of dichotomy and unreservedly rejected the changes that had occurred:

> I describe the changes that have overcome FE as managerialism. We have adopted a code of practices that we think are businesslike because, you know, the ethos is that we have to become businesslike and so we've taken these things off the shelf and I just reject that because I teach business studies and I know that the ideas that are in circulation are in fact all essentially very old fashioned . . . you know, we're 10 to 15 years behind in the sorts of processes that we're trying to develop. With the upshot that you begin to think, 'Well, why are people doing that? What is it all about?' and, even if it's not conscious, you know, there is a sort of a functional necessity, namely, to contain the system and it's exactly that – control. I find that depressing. It's to do with the way we operate. I mean, the example is we have devolved budgets. Absolute cock! We do not do anything. An example, talking to a fellow programme manager yesterday, we had a question – we want a technician. Personnel tell us we can only advertise in one newspaper so the programme manager says, 'My experience is we did it last time and we got no applications. We need two.'
> 'You can't do it.'
> 'I'll pay for it.'
> ''You can't.'
> 'I'll pay for it myself out of my own pocket – £15 in another newspaper saying, "See advert in *The Bugle*".'
> 'You can't do it. It'll set a precedent.'
> So here we are – programme manager, devolved budget – cannot spend his own money because a senior manager tells him it will set a precedent and he can't do it and . . . at the end of the day we have a budget of about £5,000 for materials and there we go. So that, you know, nothing's devolved. Everything is controlled tightly from the top and, as I say, it's like a police state.

The last statement is obviously an exaggeration, though we have already heard from SMT members who called the FEFC funding method 'Stalinist' and we interviewed teachers who described management as 'fascistic'. Yet what we are witnessing here is the limited devolution of responsibility: there is a programme budget but there is also a local rule about the placement and numbers of advertisements. This is indeed not so different from the old bureaucracy at County Hall which used to organize such advertising for its colleges with its own budget and regulations. But now that the future existence of a college is dependent on the maximization of funding from the FEFC and on the effective careful management of those funds, it is not surprising to find that strategic decisions are taken 'at the centre' and that these are passed for local implementation to middle managers in their specialist curriculum areas. This is one of the sources of the new managerialism in further education.

The Senior Management Team from their position see the need for effective management of all college procedures since they all have cost and/or funding-generation implications. The role of middle managers is central to this change toward direction from the centre since it is they who have to explain its implications and implement its detail. As we have already noted, in practice this means persuading staff who already feel themselves overburdened to do more and to do things differently; in brief, to do what, often, they do not want to do.

Another common perception shared by interviewees in each layer of the flattened hierarchy was that those above felt that they were acting to protect or shelter those below them from the demands placed upon them by the layer above them. 'That sort of mechanism is a sponge', explained a programme manager, characteristically seeing his own position as being in the worst possible situation. As a result, as he said, 'middle managers get the shit from the top and the shit from the bottom'. For they also had to 'absorb', as he put it, the reactions of teaching staff to management proposals, although he conceded, 'The A-Ps are there to do the same' in relation to the Principal.

We have also seen Principals similarly acting in what they saw as the best interest of the college as a whole by the way they adapted to the external demands of the FEFC. For example, the Principal of Inner City College declared that at incorporation: 'The goal I set myself was that staff and students shouldn't notice. I tried to insulate them and keep them beavering away in the classroom. My hope was that they would not notice, to keep them encapsulated, not to freak people . . .' (Indeed, it can be suggested that the FEFC acted similarly to protect 'its' colleges from Treasury demands and so had, to the time of writing, prevented the numbers of predicted closures and mergers of colleges, if not redundancies and retirements of teachers.)

Thus, middle managers felt it incumbent upon them to interpret SMT strategy in the best interest of teachers in their curriculum areas or Schools. As another said, 'People at programme manager level cushion or filter out a lot of the changes.' Essentially, the changes which these staff are commenting on can be traced back to the FEFC which has as one of its objectives the effective management of all resources at college level. For, where the Average Level of Funding per unit is being reduced through the working of the funding method, existing structures and allocations of responsibilities, including staffing levels, are constantly under review with one possible aim and consequence – to do the same work, or more, for less. This is a situation in which a teacher promoted into middle management can feel uncomfortable as s/he is caught between their former close colleagues and senior managers and their imperatives.

Meanwhile, at each 'layer', those below typically feel that external demands are merely being passed on to them and do not appreciate the efforts that those above feel they are making on their behalf. This does not imply that superordinates were self-deluding in their claims to protect their subordinates. As one middle-management interviewee stated,

> My greatest aim, my biggest aim is to take a load off the teachers, having been there myself. When the FEFC changes all these systems that you've got to respond to, the immediate response is to get the teachers to do it. We need information on this, we need information on that, which is necessary because you haven't got any systems in place for a while. But the whole thrust of what the Registry, MIS and the A-Ps have been doing is to get a load off, get the systems in place so that we can then provide them with the data, rather than them provide

us with the data . . . now with the new Individual Student Records we are keeping more things centrally . . . You can now click on to the student, look up, find the status of all their students on screen – 'withdrawn', 'transferred', if they're still attending, by course, by subject. You know, it's quite good now – if they had a computer to look on but there might only be one or two in a staffroom of eight people – but that's just a matter of time I suppose before we get everybody one.

In time therefore, 'when things settle down' in the perennial phrase, this middle-management interviewee felt that the College was moving towards a system in which:

All the teachers do is teach and prepare and mark and there's a whole raft of people behind them doing all the business to push more of the work towards admin. It's actually cost-effective of course. It's cheaper than to employ teachers. If you could free up more time for teachers to do what they're supposed to be doing, and what they believe they are supposed to be doing as well, they'd do it better. That's got to be cost-effective. If they do it better you've got more students. You've got more results.

This may have been the ideal and it might become attainable with more technology but we will see that, at least at the time we interviewed members of the colleges' staff, there were unanimous complaints from the main-grade teachers that the administrative load was overwhelming and they were drowning under paperwork. Teachers also resented people who had moved from their ranks into what was now largely administration. These were people like the full-time co-ordinator quoted above who confessed to us, 'I'm not displeased that I'm not teaching any more.'

Another widespread opinion of the main-grade teachers was that the numbers of administrative and clerical staff had increased disproportionately since incorporation and that these bureaucrats were drawing resources from the fundamental teaching activity of the institution, even if they saw themselves – as above – dedicated to helping it. This complaint is justified in the sense that, as we have said, on their removal from local authority support systems, the colleges had to appoint staff expert in areas such as financial control, personnel and estates management. This was not simply taking over these responsibilities from the LEAs to reduplicate them in each individual college because the actual administrative requirements, in addition, had also been increased as a result of the demands made by the FEFC funding method.

While senior managers see the urgent need for prompt and complete responses to the Funding Council, this is not necessarily so visible to the main-grade lecturers. Hence the perception that, as in the health service, the additional non-teaching staff employed to carry out these duties are an expensive consequence of the new system and divert scarce resources from the main business of learning – the teaching of students. Perhaps in time, as interviewees above hoped, a clearer understanding of the necessity for this expenditure on administration will permeate down to all teaching staff. It is possible too that the full-time co-ordinator quoted above may be proved correct in that these staff, together with the use of new technology, may remove some of the administrative burden from teachers. Teachers will then be freed to do what they all said they felt they did best and best liked to do – concentrate on students and their learning.

Communication between middle managers and the SMT was not all one-way of course. At both colleges, curriculum/programme managers and Heads of School told us that they could always talk to their Principals, though in one case the interviewee doubted if he was always listened to. Teachers expressed similar reservations about the colleges' formal processes of consultation and even the SMT voiced concerns in Chapter Three about FEFC consultation exercises, p. 43. Also, we have already seen (on p. 53, for instance) that at both colleges senior managers appreciated the stress and intensification of labour endured by many of their staffs. However, the SMT also felt that these extra burdens, which they laboured under themselves, were worth taking on for the sake of the college's immediate and future survival, as well as for the improvements in quality which they all felt had been achieved. They thought that as a result of the changes they had introduced, teachers felt a new responsibility for work over which they had more control and that they enjoyed a greater self-respect for doing a better job because the service to students had improved.

None of the main-grade lecturers or their line managers that we spoke to endorsed such a vision. Middle managers though were more likely to agree with more parts of it, for instance:

> I think the students get a far better deal. The facilities we're now offering for trainees here is much better whereas there just used to be a person who came in because there were so many of them after training we didn't have to advertise. We closed the door whenever we felt like it. We had to provide nothing other than the basic necessities. That's changed.

All main-grade lecturers interviewed also agreed there had been some changes for the better. They might also concede under questioning that 'the good old days' were not in fact so perfect as they might nostalgically appear in retrospect. The balance between such concessions to the new ethos varied systematically amongst interviewees in the way we have suggested by age, experience (length of service) and subject specialism. We shall therefore now examine the responses of main-grade lecturers at both colleges divided along this spectrum of opinion.

Going down a level

There was some indication, though it cannot be more than indicative given that our selection of interviewees was too small to be as representative as a wider sample would have been, that bore out the opinion of the Assistant Principal above that staff attitudes were changing as 'It seems to be going down a level a year.' So that, as one lecturer opined,

> Once the system settles down . . . I think loyalty will come and I think you'll find, you know, they'll have to accept a certain amount of the painful stuff that happened in the health service and things like that. I hate it. I resent it profoundly. I find it offensive. It makes me angry. But you have to accept it. I think it's just a long change span.

After all, she added, 'It's about change in culture really and responses to people's idea of what they see the work as being. I think it's a massive culture change . . .'

We shall return in our concluding chapter on the future of further education to the discussion of the possibility that, as new staff join FE who have never experienced any other way of doing things, the changes brought about by incorporation, the new funding regime and new curricula will all come to be accepted as normal. For now, it is worth noting that the older age profile of the staff at Inner City College – the longest-serving lecturer interviewed was in his 32nd year of teaching – in part explained the more negative opinions of most teachers there. At Home Counties, where the age profile was more mixed and all lecturers were on the new contract, there was not the bitterness and division that persisted at Inner City. These were apparent there because teachers were divided in working to different conditions of service, for example with regard to maximum weekly and annual teaching hours. Those on the old contract, of course, had received no increase in pay since 1993. This was another reason that morale seemed higher at Home Counties than Inner City.

As more than one Home Counties interviewee commented, especially in comparison with elsewhere in FE, 'I think, having spoken to other people who work in different colleges, we've actually been very fortunate here. I think staff morale is generally quite good.' Even if there was still a feeling that, as another interviewee said, 'You come to Home Counties to die', this was not only because it was hard to move elsewhere but also because it had a good reputation, not only amongst teachers but also with parents and students in the locality, and was in a 'nice' area in which to work.

At both colleges, several interviewees – again depending upon age, experience and position – recognized that their respective Principals had been instrumental in one case in creating a new college and in the other virtually recreating an old one. As one Inner City Head of School put it, 'In one sense any pain is worth that if it leads to a situation where the institution is guaranteed survival.' While another said, 'I know this is just between you and me but, I mean, the Principal's been very good in a lot of ways for this college. I mean, we've had some rubbish here you know over the years. She has turned this place around, no two ways about it.' This was also acknowledged by main-grade lecturers at Inner City, who considered the Principal had 'arrested a cycle of decline', so that 'it's a different place to what it was five or six years ago' and 'we're starting to believe maybe we've got a chance'. At Home Counties one lecturer commented:

> The main reason I signed [the new contract] really is because of the threat at the time that the college would be – I can't remember the term they used – it could have been ratecapped, where they keep back a certain proportion of their funding [i.e. 'clawback', see p. 20]. They [the government and FEFC] said if staff didn't sign the contract by a certain date then they would hold back something like five per cent of the budget, so for me that was a real motivating factor in signing it. Plus the consultation that took place, the changes in the contract after discussions with the unions etc., plus I do have a lot of respect really for the Principal and his principles.

Yet, even with staff who were largely supportive of management, there was the feeling at both colleges that:

> It's very much more distanced from management now. Certainly senior management and even on the programme manager level I think there seems to be a very big gap between being a main-grade lecturer and the next jump which is programme manager here and there's very few promotion prospects really, which I think for a lot of people can be quite problematic. You know, the motivation and the looking ahead, you haven't got the same prospects at all as you had before incorporation . . .

This foreshortening of career prospects, as we called it in Chapter 3 (p. 51), was a consequence of 'delayering' the old hierarchy to form the new 'flattened hierarchy'. These new flattened hierarchies had a 'very big gap' between core SMT and workforce, bridged only by remaining middle managers.

Younger staff and others recently appointed were less likely to experience this career frustration – yet, perhaps, like new students entering the system for the first time, they accepted the new arrangements as normal and also more readily granted:

> Some things are better for students . . . some of the pastoral systems, for example, the college has set up are actually very supportive. One of the good things that's come out of the FEFC is the enormous amounts of money that are available for additional needs. Students in our college have benefited enormously from that. Some of the students I teach have had up to an hour a week individual tuition on top of their course. We couldn't afford that in the past so that would be one of the improvements I could point to.

This acknowledgement also depended upon the teaching specialism of interviewees so that a learning support lecturer for instance, reflected:

> I think in the last few years it's better for students in some ways. In theory they have access into – for my students anyway – into mainstream courses, and that is improving. It's not such a hard fight to get them in but it's a harder fight to keep them there because the receiving teachers haven't got that same level of commitment, they haven't got the time either . . . In terms of the physical, the capital expenditure, yes it's much better.

This last point was admitted by all interviewees. Such endorsements of what SMT had told us were also more readily conceded, as might be expected, from teachers whose students had not only benefitted, as had special needs above, but also from staff whose subjects had received substantial capital investment. For example:

> . . . compared to, on a vocational course like information technology, the old BTEC National was very out of date. The syllabus was written something like, um, I don't know, the early 1980s – and it hadn't changed since then. When we used to have

moderators come in we used to say, 'We really can't teach this syllabus. It's completely out of date.' So the new GNVQ course is great. It's really up to date. So in terms of teaching it, it's very interesting [and] I think the students respond to it very well because it's all windows-based stuff. We've got fairly state-of-the-art software and so they respond very well to that and they can see that it's what's being used out in business. You know, there's lots of stuff in the papers about the Internet and Windows 95 and so it's clear that we are up to date with what's going on.

Despite these improvements the interviewee above continued:

The workload has increased substantially over the last two or three years. Part of that is because I'm very involved with GNVQ, and GNVQ workload is definitely higher than it was before. [But, she added] We're doing more hours anyway because it's a new contract [and in addition], The classes are bigger this year. So, it's just more pressure being put on.

For no matter how much main-grade lecturers endorsed improvements since incorporation, they all commented on the extra work that the changes had meant for them. For instance, even a newly appointed lecturer in business studies who recognized and agreed with the changed administration of the college, feeling that it was 'more professional', described teaching 25 hours a week as 'a nightmare'. Also involved in GNVQ, the time that he had to spend in administration and preparation of his courses meant that he had no time to deal with students individually:

They stop you in the corridors. They are always coming into the room and they need help and you can't really say, 'Look, I'm too busy. I've got too much workload. I can't really deal with you now, go away.' After all, the main purpose of one being here is to provide assistance to students, to provide an education for students. So they come first, if you like, as far as I'm concerned.

New though he was to further education, this interviewee espoused the service ethic in which students come first. This dedication to the needs of students was, we have seen, shared by the college managers who tried to deliver it more effectively through the new market mechanisms. The ethos of service to students and the community was also central to the self-conceptions and purposes of FE as articulated by a whole raft of staff who had been in the sector for a long time, were not in expanding areas of provision, had seen an increase and not a decrease in their teaching load and who therefore rejected most of the changes since incorporation and the market approach to the business of learning with which they were associated.

Even for those who in part welcomed the changes:

I don't think you can run an FE college like a business. It shouldn't be a business at all. We should be offering a service to the community and responding to the needs that they have got. Not when they state a need and we say, 'How many units is this going to attract?' [because] we're all very aware of how many units are attracted by certain courses and it's very much finance driven.

The increased workload was not resented for itself but because it detracted from what interviewees saw as the essential public service that the college was supposed to provide. It also had other consequences, as this lecturer went on:

> We don't have any social time at all. We don't take a lunch hour. It's all, you know, you're busy from the moment you arrive to the moment you leave. There is very little time that we spend outside college at all. You don't sit around talking to people; you just haven't got time to do that any more. Whereas things were much more leisurely I think in the past; although I think we're probably going back more than five or six years now but the job compared to, say, ten years ago is probably unrecognizable. [As a result], Job satisfaction isn't really there as much because you've got too much to do. You never get everything done and you never get it done – well, 'never' is a bit dramatic – you often don't get it done satisfactorily.

At Inner City a lecturer told us: 'Some teachers that I work with are in tears and I get tearful some days. It's not because we're neurotic or whatever. It's because it's bloody hard work.' While at Home Counties another confessed:

> I have never worked as hard in my life and as long hours in a day, so many days in a week and I can't see it getting any better and I find that quite intolerable in some respects because I don't see how it's going to be possible to put boundaries around the expectation because of the drive for productivity as far as I can see. I mean, I just see it as a continual push for more work out of fewer staff really, so part of that is around a slight reduction in the number of full-time staff but also in an increase in expectation in terms of what we're supposed to be doing. And a lot of it's administration – it's not teaching. No, what's causing the work is not the teaching for me. What's causing the work is the effects of trying to put lots and lots of systems in place, trying to bring everything together in some way and have it much more managed and monitored and more accountable.

This confirmed the estimation of one of the programme managers, who was the immediate 'line manager' of the main-grade lecturer quoted above, that 'the accountability of teachers has changed'. This was, he added, a 'dramatic change':

> I don't suppose the past was exactly the situation where if all students passed their exams you were a good teacher and if they all failed they were bad students but I have a role here managing the A-level programme where, after the exam results come out, I interview every A-level co-ordinator to question them about their results for that year. So I spend most of this term having meetings with them, examining last year's results. Why were they different from the year before? How were they different? What happened? What changed? How are you going to improve it next year?

As compared with the past:

> I don't think people would have been accountable in the same way. I mean, I'm
> sure heads of departments used to give people rollickings in the past if their exam
> results blipped up or down in a bad way. But it's much more systematic now.

In addition to the 'much more systematic' monitoring and accountability of
lecturers, confirmed by her line manager, the lecturer quoted above continued:

> There is also the sense that we're having to spend more and more time supporting
> our students who are also not unaffected by the economic climate and various
> other things that are going on. So that's not about teaching either; that's about the
> kind of work you have to do outside the teaching to support students that are
> there. The kind of teaching again that concentrates a lot on teams means that you
> have to make a lot of time for meetings. There are endless numbers of meetings.

At both colleges the demands from new types and larger numbers of students,
along with changes to the curriculum and assessment regimes which require new ways
of working in teams, and matrix management structures necessitate 'endless' formal
meetings. Meetings that many interviewees (including members of the SMT) feel are
often 'meetings for the sake of meetings'. Interviewees also noted an erosion of the ethic
of public service and its replacement by a business ethic, plus an increase in
administration resulting from the more systematic monitoring of students by lecturers
and of lecturers by their line managers, not to mention the constant and increasing
pressure to deliver more for less. But there was also something else about the new
working practices that bothered the colleges' staffs, something that for one Inner City
lecturer was not so easy to define:

> There is a loss in terms of, I don't know . . . something really deep and internal
> hasn't happened. It hasn't been done. In terms of actually looking at staff and the
> way resources are managed . . . The 'we' ethic is not there and that stems out of, I
> don't know, feelings of insecurity. If people are persistently feeling insecure in
> terms of the work they are doing – next year, God it might change again! GNVQs
> going to change again and different types of pressures which are because of
> market forces or whatever and you are part of this market force because you
> become the product. We're not perfect products. Some aren't bloody BMWs, you
> know! I don't pretend to be.

This combined feeling of individual stress and insecurity was paradoxical because, as the
interviewee above said, in comparison with 'the old days', 'now it's taking into account
the whole of the college. And it's not necessarily true that wasn't happening before but
the sense of one's voice in terms of managing and power actually becomes quite
different.'

Many staff were not morally involved in the enterprise, as SMT hoped they would
become, but actually felt more divided and isolated from each other, both by pressure of

work, as well as by underlying feelings of insecurity. They felt that they could not measure up to the pressures of increased accountability that had been put upon them. As a Home Counties lecturer summed it up:

> It's a creaking system only held together by the work of the people there and that is a depressing picture. There will be another picture that says, 'Well, people who can't cope with it can get out and other people come in who can cope with it.' That's the other model, isn't it? I think I'm one of the creaking ones, that's the problem.

The feeling that they were 'creaking' under the strain and 'aren't bloody BMWs' drove these staff, who in many ways welcomed the changes that had occurred and were optimistically seen by management as 'the next level down' to accept them, towards the camp of the mass of their colleagues who at Inner City had not signed the new contract and who at both colleges defined themselves in a defensive and persecuted opposition to further change. The move to the ranks of the disenchanted resolved the conflict that we have seen was felt also at the level of both Principals and 'schizophrenic' SMT as well as by middle managers. Uncertainties could be jettisoned for an unambiguous identification as 'marginal performers' (see below) as was illustrated by main-grade interviewees who were proud to place themselves in this category.

The marginal performers

Clearly this term, picked up from management literature and ironically applied to themselves, did not mean that these interviewees thought that they did less work than anybody else. In fact, like the interviewees above, it was central to their view of affairs that their basic work of teaching sustained the colleges and was the essential business of learning that was only obscured and interrupted by management innovations and government interference, particularly the marketing of education and training. For example:

> I think the best way I can put it for you is something which sums it all up as a product of the changes since 1993, the post-incorporation ethos. A couple of months ago I was given a flyer with the title 'The Marginal Performer' and it was a flyer for a training course directed at my line manager, people like Heads of School, and what this course said was that it was designed to enable managers to deal with the marginal performer. And the marginal performer was defined in this flyer as somebody who had not embraced the market approach and still had a social service ethos. And so I regard myself still as proud to be a marginal performer. I think I ought to go around with a badge on, you know. But I mean that really sums things up. What is fundamental to that is change in the funding methodology. Basically, we are getting each year 90 per cent of the funding for the previous year and my view may be a kind of economic reductionism but everything flows from that.

While for this interviewee, 'My loyalty has never been to the College anyway. It's been to the students and to the profession, the discipline, and to the union as well, not necessarily in that order.' He still conceded there had been some improvements – 'There is capital spending going on', for instance. But he contested that money was being spent to best effect. Instead of what he regarded as cosmetic refurbishments, for example, 'those thousands of pounds should have gone to relieve student poverty', or to part-time lecturers 'who are anything up to £10 per hour worse off as a result of changes since 1993'. 'It's not that I don't think that changes were needed. Changes have always been needed.' But in the absence of increased funding, and with a constantly reducing unit of resource, he rejected any further changes.

As a colleague added, there had already been too many changes and this was part of the problem:

> My general impressions of what's been happening over the past few years are a multitude of initiatives, ideas and new directions which tend to in fact come thick and fast and are not properly looked into, investigated and realized before you move on to the next directive or idea . . . A lot of these ideas are good ideas – one's not against them in terms of the direction and their logic, but it's the constant introduction of one initiative after another without the ability to work it through. [As a result], I think myself and many of my colleagues – in fact, probably the majority of colleagues if they are honest – are in a state of some considerable fatigue and levels of morale are very low, not because one disagrees with the initiatives but one basically is sceptical about the sincerity and efficiency with which these initiatives are put into practice.

In addition, very often lecturers who had been teaching the same courses for many years saw little point in the changes that were being urged upon them from above: 'A lot of the changes that have happened was 180 degrees change really when you come to think of it but I haven't changed anything I've been doing so many years because I thought I'd been doing it so well there is no point in changing or reforming.' This was not just complacency. Lecturers related at length their concerns with falling standards. They attributed these not only to new qualifications and curricula and the changed nature of the new student body, which they saw as demanding more help and support from them, but they were also concerned to meet their own idea of what they considered was required of students as engineers – or chefs, or builders, or hairdressers, in short to whichever standard in whichever vocational area they were teaching. It was important to their own self-esteem and professional identity that these standards were maintained, even if they were no longer technically required, either by the new forms of competence-based assessment or by actual practice in the trade for which they prepared students. For teachers of academic subjects, as well as getting their students through their exams, it was of corresponding importance to impart also a general and critical awareness that was not confined to their particular subject of study but helped students make connection with other subjects and other areas of their lives. Yet the new conditions of their work made it, many interviewees felt, increasingly difficult to achieve these goals that were so vital to their professional identity as traditionally conceived, so that the job became 'not what I went into teaching to do'.

Each new initiative being announced by a flurry of memoranda, initiative fatigue focused upon what we referred to in Chapter 3 as 'management by memo'. This was a consequence, we have argued, of the new reorganizations and the gap that had opened up in the new flattened hierarchy or matrix between workers and core management. At both colleges interviewees repeatedly complained of 'massive amounts of paperwork', 'reams of paper cascading', 'the same sort of mindless kind of data – it's a joke to everybody', 'monitoring things on an absurd sort of level'. So: 'People go to their pigeon holes with a heavy heart because you know there's going to be another seven new pieces of paper saying this, that and the other and the amount of paper that's generated in terms of directives and all the rest of it.' As another lecturer said, 'That paper goes into the bin. I mean, I look at it but it goes into the bin. It annoys me just picking it up and putting it in the bin. It doesn't do anything to me. I don't think it does to most of the people.'

This was linked by interviewees to the increase in administration over teaching staff which we have discussed. From the perspective of the lecturer above: 'If you employ 20 administrators, every administrator in the college has got to produce and do his job or her job, has got to produce paper, has got to tell you what he's doing and help and improve your facilities or your way of doing things.' And from another at the other college, answering his own question about what SMT actually did: 'My impression is they work very hard' to produce 'a lot of paper' and 'the sum result' of all this activity as far as he was concerned was 'lots of paper, lots of draft memos and, well, drafts of policies and the sixth draft of policies and so on.' This view of management was clearly very different from that which senior and middle managers had of themselves.

Similarly, many main-grade lecturers disagreed with management's estimation that quality had been improved or at least been maintained while being extended to more students. By contrast:

> I would say that the actual quality of teaching and therefore the quality of what we offer has declined dramatically . . . The curriculum offer for students is far worse. It is narrower in some ways because the actual range of the offer has decreased. We've withdrawn from many vocational areas of course. In terms of staff/student contact that has reduced fairly dramatically and because of the engine of the funding mechanism the college is recruiting inappropriately to courses thereby affecting retention. Students are joining courses, finding that their course is not appropriate, above their level of ability – it's just not the thing for them – and they are then withdrawing or just dropping out, occasionally transferring to another course but very little transfer goes on.

Likewise the consultation processes which management had insisted on were widely regarded by many at the whiteboard face as 'a charade', 'just pretending consultation', 'talking to a brick wall' and, echoing the middle manager above (p. 63), 'consultation doesn't mean listening'. Again, this repeated not only what a middle manager had told us but what SMT had said about the FEFC and its consultations of the Henry Ford type, the obvious answer being Option E, 'so you all fill in Option E' (p. 43). For lecturing staff the equivalent was 'If you sign the new contract, you get the rise. If you don't sign, you don't get it.' Now the only contact – except for the memos from management they all complained about and occasional full staff meetings ('basically college management addressing staff') – that such lecturers had with SMT was via their immediate line, or programme manager: 'We are accountable for everything. We are directly connected to our manager, aren't we? We don't talk to the senior managers up there on the third floor. We have nothing to say to them.'

In many of these comments teachers are referring to the impact on their working lives and the effect on their dealings with students of what they see as the excessive demands made upon them by the management of the new system. In the past, FE teachers – like school and university teachers – had considerable autonomy in their teaching. For both school and FE, if not yet for higher education, this has changed with interventions by central government into both curriculum and assessment. The National Curriculum and the introduction of tests at ages 7, 11, 14 as well as 16 has transformed the lives of school teachers. The parallel for FE teachers has been GNVQs with their course-work assessment and recording of detailed competences.

At the same time, the policies of the FEFC and its requirements for data on student enrolment, retention and achievement have led also to procedures for checking on each of these at the level of the teaching team and the individual teacher. Hence the cry of 'management by memo' as either the MIS officer or the programme leader requests more and more information. The effect has been to reduce the space and scope for the exercise of teachers' professional autonomy, admittedly an underdeveloped notion in further education where not all lecturers hold teacher qualifications. For a common element in these statements by teachers is the loss of control over much of their working lives and the feeling that they are increasingly regulated either from outside (as by the NCVQ) or indirectly by systems locally created in response to the requirements of the FEFC.

To go back to the old situation pre-incorporation appeared attractive to many and clinging on to old certainties partly accounts for the apparent complacency and conservatism of some of their comments above. However, many interviewees also recognized that there were things wrong with 'the good old days' and that to go back to them was impossible in any case. Yet there seemed no alternative way forward to the route charted for them by management. Faced with this situation, 'People don't know what to do. They're snookered.' Dissent was disorganized. The collapse of community with the reorganization and reduction of the old departments and in the staffroom where staff no longer enjoyed common break-times but individuals were now isolated and differently accountable for the various aspects of their work was mirrored outside the college by the competition and isolation of one college pitted against another locally and on a national level by local wage bargaining. Several interviewees lamented the resulting lack of collective response and effective leadership from their union NATFHE in the long-running contracts dispute, just as managers regretted the lack of a national body to speak on behalf of the FE sector as a whole.

To these feelings of isolation and insecurity was added paranoia. People did not like to complain publicly, as more than one interviewee told us, because their position and that of the college depended so much upon market image that 'if there's a hint of anything that could be leaked to the press', 'if this leaks out those up there at the top will think that this person has been spreading this kind of thing'. As a result, 'You're constantly looking at your back . . . and so it's rare that any public expression of this dissatisfaction is ever seen. But informally of course it goes on all the time.'

There could be a number of reactions to this situation that our interviewees considered and to an extent enacted in their daily responses to it. The option of becoming managers themselves was rejected by interviewees, who we have already seen were frustrated by the decrease in possibilities for career progression offered by the new structures. Several also mentioned that the extra work and responsibility involved in becoming a programme manager or Head of School was not worth the two or three thousand-pound increase they would receive in salary. Interviewees also worried that FE salaries overall were now falling behind those of school teachers, reversing their previous superiority. They associated this with a further decline in the status of the sector.

An alternative reaction by individuals was one of accommodation and withdrawal mentioned to us by interviewees at both colleges:

> As more and more your job turns into a job people didn't come into teaching to do, it turns [it] into, well, I'll come in, do my hours and go home and I'll cut down on my marking and I'll cut my essay-setting, which is the thing that's going to get my students through their exams – exam practice. I'll start saying to students 'No' when I would previously say 'Yes'. I'll start saying to students 'I haven't got time to see you out of lessons' and consequently you start thinking about yourself more rather than thinking about your students which is why we should all be here obviously. And so the meaning of the job is reduced . . . Here the staff are relatively old and most of them are saying, 'Oh well . . . bugger it! Look after myself.'

So younger staff looked around for alternative employment outside education, while older ones sought early retirement as long as this was still on offer. For example, 'I'm basically tired and weary of it all and I would just like to get out and there are many people who feel the same way . . .'

Where staff were strongly unionized along traditional lines, as at Inner City, they could react collectively to the pressures upon them. As their union representative said, 'I mean, it's worth remembering that there is a major contract dispute on at the moment. People like myself have not had a pay increase for three years running as a result of this contract dispute. That had resulted in three days' strike action during the FEFC inspection last session. So it shows you how strong the feeling is.' This of course contested the notion of a professional as someone who did not take strike action but, with the loss of autonomy associated with the professional ideal, it confirmed the belief of active trade unionists that they were white-collar workers rather than professionals. They rejected new notions of autonomous professionals as 'reflective practitioners', seeing this 'rhetoric of accountability' as merely 'delegating the responsibility to cut'.

The 'new unionism' was embodied to an extent in the NATFHE branch at Home Counties, where, as was explained to us, 'Everybody's got new contracts from the Principal down to the part-time cleaners.' In effect, this accepted also the new self-accountable professionalism of reflective practice and therefore confined the union to professional advocacy and consultation with management, though in this college too the numbers of grievances taken up by the union had increased since incorporation. To both union branches, the public service ethic of quality provision for their students and the community was as central to their members' declared concerns as was the complementary struggle to maintain working conditions.

Principals and their SMTs hoped that they could by astute management reconcile running the corporate college more efficiently and the values of the service ethic both they and their staffs espoused. For their part, middle managers were simultaneously pulled in two directions at once in their everyday practice of mediation across the sharpened divide between staff and management that re-organization had entailed within the corporate college. The resulting feelings of ambivalence we have seen were only partially shared at a further layer down but they were rejected by those like the interviewee above who defined themselves as 'marginal performers'.

Differences between interviewees focused upon what main-grade lecturers said about the changes taking place with respect to teaching and learning methods. The reduction in teaching hours is coupled with the increases reported to us in the size of many teaching groups (although the FEFC records no overall increases in class sizes). This adds to the pressures on teachers as they work to do justice for their students by ensuring that they are thoroughly prepared for the various forms of assessment used in different programmes on the three main academic, general vocational and work-based pathways. To do this for the new students now in further education, many teachers have adopted new teaching methods, more centred on individual students and involving the individual negotiation of learning plans and independent study of topics for assignments, for example. All these new forms of learning take more of the teacher's time, and with less time available and larger groups their quality is increasingly jeopardized. As an Inner City lecturer emphasized, 'the new approaches are far more demanding. It's the easiest thing in the world to chalk and talk.'

For this and other reasons, to help ease the pressure – in both Home Counties and Inner City, as in many other colleges – we have seen Resource-Based Learning Centres created. These develop the functions of the college library enhanced by the addition of learning materials for A-level modules or GNVQ units which enable students to work individually or in small groups on topics which would have been previously taught in class sessions. New information and communication technologies also enable students to work independently through individual learning programmes and to produce assignments in computerized formats. We have already remarked this shift to Resource-Based Learning (RBL) at both colleges in Chapter 3. Despite its cost, it is seen by management as a sound educational investment in the context of reductions in teacher time and larger numbers of students following more varied and diverse courses.

So far, there is no evidence that student achievement is adversely affected by this innovation but many teachers regretted the change. For example, 'I wouldn't say nothing has changed but I think that often the changes are very minor in terms of the basic objective of improving the situation for students. For example, you create a new learning centre and in doing so you destroy a library.' His colleague described the ideology associated with RBL as 'absolutely spurious':

I mean the thinking that we are now seen as learning managers rather than teachers – we're facilitating learning – and the sort of hands-on approach where we were actually there engaging people is very much on the back foot these days. There is a massive increase in investment in Resource-Based Learning for example . . . I think it's a worse deal for the students because contact between students and staff is much reduced and at this level that is very important. It's also reduced because staff time is being consumed on a mass of administrative stuff. Staff are into just grabbing a worksheet and just walking into a room. That side of things just can't be exaggerated.

We have said enough to show that, unsurprisingly perhaps, the view of management in the previous chapter did not accord with the view of staff in both colleges, even if the management view had penetrated at least in part to middle managers and even to some staff in new and expanding areas. The majority however were still unaffected in their attitudes, particularly amongst the larger numbers of older staff at Inner City, where, in addition, departmental organization on different sites survived in modified form. It has been seen also that those at the whiteboard face who actually deliver the teaching, while they recognized some improvements, contradicted management estimation of improvement in the quality of student experience. We now therefore turn to the students themselves to find out what they made of the business of learning at the two colleges.

Chapter 5

The students' experience

A youth's story is relatively unusual. Rare. For some reason, we seem wary of hoisting our little snippets upon the general ear. It smacks of precocity, hubris, wilful ignorance. What could we have had in our short lives worth hearing about? Who wants to know? We don't have access to that trunk of years, that big bag of witnessed time. This is our handicap and our strength. Events mean more to the young. We lack the objective splay and pose of sequence. Our past is immediate, episodic, hotly self-obsessed. And above all – visual, pictorial. Comprised of sense and free of much judgement or clouding thought. Our past has that focused, hard-eyed strength. Detail, accuracy, vividness. This is what the memories of the young possess.

Robert McLiam Wilson, *Ripley Bogle*

The new students in the colleges

Having examined the contrasting perceptions of managers and teachers at our two colleges, we turn next to the students who are the objects and beneficiaries, if not the customers or clients, for whom the business of learning is conducted at Home Counties and Inner City Colleges. The aim of the chapter is to report on their experience, which is too often forgotten, or appears only incidental to many studies of further education. It can then be evaluated alongside that of their teachers in our conclusion.

FE colleges traditionally catered for younger workers but today about half of all students in FE colleges nationally, excluding those in sixth-form colleges, are over 26, less than one third 16–18 and the average age of all students at Inner City College was 28. Nevertheless, most full-time students are younger and at both of our colleges many staff commonly referred to students collectively as 'the kids'. We have seen from our interviews with the Principals of our two colleges how they aimed their main full-time provision at different groups of students – from school-leavers at Home Counties to those who were older at Inner City. These different strategies not only reflect the two main types of FE and tertiary college but also afford, we have suggested, alternative possible futures for FE in the UK.

Apart from the differences in the age, race, social and educational background of their student bodies, our two colleges in their very different circumstances and environments differed in many other ways. At both places the business of learning extended to other activities that heightened the contrast between the two colleges, with different arrangements for and numbers of access and overseas students, various links to industry and franchising, for example. Indeed, we have already remarked in Chapter 1 on the variety of FE that makes it impossible to find representative colleges that typify a sector characterized by its range and variety of provision, or even to find sufficient similarities to compare like with like.

We wanted to convey a picture of learning and teaching in two contrasted colleges that gives readers some sense of what is happening in FE today. We therefore concentrated on the central business of learning at the two colleges – the three main pathways which are the mainstream work of further education institutions. Matched groups of students on academic classroom, general vocational workshop and work-based 'pathways' – as the government now calls them – at Advanced, Intermediate and Foundation levels (corresponding to NVCQ levels 3, 2 and 1) at both colleges were therefore selected in the manner described for the selection of staff whose views have been presented in previous chapters. The presidents of the student unions in both colleges were also interviewed.

Overall enrolment by the levels of learning from which students were selected were as follows:

	Home Counties	Inner City
Foundation	3%	21%
Intermediate	54%	39%
Advanced	35%	32%
Higher	8%	8%

As explained, there was a division of labour between the two authors; while one was interviewing the teachers the other talked to their students. As the latter had previously been engaged in a study of higher education, he began his interviews by talking to those most similar to many of the HE students he had just interviewed by introducing himself to classes at both colleges in their second year of sociology A-level and GCSE sociology students in the second term of their one-year course. (Also because he could then make a contribution to their exam work by advising students on their project investigations and talking to them about the sociology of education.) BTEC National Diploma and First Diploma Engineers (corresponding to NCVQ levels 3 and 2) were then interviewed at both colleges, along with Association for Accounting Technicians at Intermediate and Foundation (confusingly equivalent to everyone else's Advanced and Intermediate, i.e. 3 and 2, levels), and finally Foundation level 1 students.

As a result of this selection of students, most interviewees were young and full time, with the exception of the mainly over-21-year-old and predominantly female accounting technicians, the majority of whom at Home Counties and about half of whom at Inner City were released from work for one day a week in the classical FE fashion (the rest at the latter college being unemployed, though many of these had previously worked in accounts). The rest of our student interviewees were straight from school in the majority of cases at Home Counties College, while those at Inner City were on average one or two years older. As would be expected, classroom-based GCSE and A-level sociology students were also overwhelmingly female, while the engineers were all males with one exceptional female interviewed in the Inner City First Diploma group. At Home Counties only two out of the group of ten Foundation level students interviewed were women, while at Inner City the group of 15 students divided eight to seven male to female and included two young mothers. Similarly, black and other minority ethnic students predominated amongst full-time students at all levels at Inner City College, while they were unusual at any level at Home Counties.

Students were interviewed either singly or in pairs, following a semi-structured schedule (see Appendix). In the latter case interviews were in general longer as interviewees sometimes discussed matters between themselves as well as with the interviewer. In the former, interviewees would sometimes voice opinions, which, comparison of the 100 or so interviews showed, they were reluctant to express in front of another student.

FE students' experience of college tends to be peculiarly instrumental and transitory, often attended only part-time and always as a means to an end, leading on to somewhere else. In many cases, students do not stay for long in FE – many on short courses for a year, or two years at the most. They tend therefore not to identify with their college in the way that school and university students may do, and colleges face the task of generating a natural community life. At most, FE students may spontaneously identify with their course, the group taking it and the lecturer who will get them through it. In many ways part of the appeal of FE to many of its students has always been that their courses were short, practical and relevant to their immediate needs. However, possibly all this is altering, along with so much else, as periods spent in further education lengthen for many students.

Possibilities of 'progression' both within and from FE are central to the comprehensive mission espoused by the sector today and by both of our colleges in relation to the communities they serve. Yet FE is not comprehensive in the same sense as comprehensive schools are. While they will take all comers, FE college students do not all follow the same curriculum and their attendance is not compulsory. Even common or core (now 'key' skills) are taught differently to different students. So, a broader curriculum offer is not the same thing as a comprehensive one. FE may be polytechnic but it is not comprehensive.

Entrants to FE from schools are sorted into Advanced, Intermediate and Foundation levels on the basis of their achievement in GCSE exams and, despite the ideal of 'progression' from one level to another, they remain largely within the pathway they have chosen – or that has been chosen for them. These pathways supposedly enjoy 'parity of esteem' but arguably the divisions between academic, vocational and work-based study reproduce the old tripartite divisions between grammar, technical and secondary modern schools at a tertiary stage. What has been called 'tertiary tripartism', rather than comprehensive tertiary provision, then segregates one type of student from another.

Indeed, the organization of these three pathways at all their levels of study, together with their characteristically different curricula (as between academic subject-based A-levels, GNVQs applicable to a general vocational area and job-specific, work-based NVQs – as outlined in Chapter 2), hamper any efforts to make them compatible and to combine them; as mentioned, two A-levels equal one GNVQ3 and one GNVQ2 equals four or five GCSEs at grades A–C, for instance. The different pathways in classrooms and laboratories, in workshops, or based in employment therefore remain largely distinct from each other at all their levels save Foundation where, as is commonly the case, they are united in an integrated programme at both colleges of classroom and workshop learning combined with work experience.

Interviewees were thus following mainly one pathway and level or another, though at both colleges some combined GCSE sociology with GNVQs 2 or 3, or with A-levels. Some Foundation students too included one or two GCSEs in their programme, or even A-level art in one case and philosophy in another. For the workshop-based engineers, both their one-year BTEC First Diploma, and the two-year National Diploma to which it was preliminary, were full-time programmes. They were tailored to fit the 21-hour rule (16 hours from October 1996) so that unemployed students over 18 years old were technically available for work in order to be in receipt of state benefits as half of all Inner City College students were. Accountancy technicians, whether in work or out, attended for only one day a week on both their one-year level 2 equivalent and two-year level 3 programmes. These were intended to relate to the work from which they were seconded in most cases at Home Counties and in some cases at Inner City. The experiences recounted in interviews with students at all three levels will therefore be presented separately.

The separation of different types of student at different levels on different pathways within the college, even if all share the common canteen and other facilities, occurs despite the efforts of both our colleges to organize optional 'electives' and other sporting and social activities additional to courses leading to qualifications in which students from different pathways can mix together. However, most students are unable and unwilling to discriminate directly between different types and level of course in terms of the various social and educational backgrounds of those following them. This was not only because the equivalence of the qualifications to which they lead is unclear; for instance, whether A-levels for entrance to higher education and the uncertainty of employment thereafter were 'better' or 'worse' than GNVQ or BTEC qualifications which for some lead to immediate and possibly more certain and secure employment.

Even the Home Counties A-level sociology students, despite covering the sociology of education in their syllabus, though they asserted that everyone on whatever course at the College was 'the same', could not explain how it happened that no one in the class actually knew, or was friends with, anyone doing hairdressing at the College, although one conceded, 'It seems that lots of people who live on the estates in Market Town have gone on to do hairdressing.' While from her knowledge of the membership of the students' snion at Home Counties, the SU president there thought gender was a more significant division by subject of study but, with 'quite a lot of males doing dance, for instance', even this was 'not highly significant'. So: 'there aren't really things like if you're this class or this type of person you therefore do this course. Everybody's treated as an equal. It doesn't make any difference what you are. I wouldn't say you get one type of person on one type of course and another on another. Everybody's mixed in OK.'

From the Foundation up

By contrast, some of the Foundation-level students, who, as explained, were interviewed last (but perhaps – with hindsight – should have been interviewed first) at both colleges, were very clear how college functioned to both differentiate between and apparently equate students at various levels on the three pathways. They saw this in relation to their previous experience of schooling, for most of them had statements of special educational need and had come to college from bridging arrangements with local special schools or had been referred to the course after unhappy experiences of mainstream schooling.

Along with the adult returners and also some of those retaking GCSEs or embarking instead upon competence-based GNVQ or BTEC courses, these Foundation-level students also illustrate most clearly the traditionally second-chance nature of FE provision – 'to catch up on what I missed from school'. More than other interviewees therefore they emphasized the differences between compulsory schooling and the two years they had enjoyed (in the main) at college.

This was explained by one student who had learning support for his statement of special educational needs throughout mainstream schooling and had not therefore been segregated, as he now was for most of his time in the Foundation group, from other students. As he said:

> I thought it would be like that – the people on other courses would look down on you – but it's not like that. That's different from school because if someone was sort of doing GCSEs at a higher level than you, they would sort of try and put you down and make you think you're really stupid, you know, but at college they don't do that. They just treat everyone equal because most people at college are older and past that stage. When you're at college and you're near the end of your course you're thinking about those sort of things – like where am I going to get a full-time job and where am I going to live and all that. 13- and 14-year-olds don't think about that for three years or so. They're not thinking they're better than you because they're going to get a better job but because they think they're cleverer than you. That's because they think they can handle it more, more difficult subjects, but it doesn't necessarily have anything to do with anything. Most people don't know what they're talking about. It's a load of gibberish. All they think about at that particular time is 'I'm on a higher course than you so I must be better than you'. I'm not saying the school didn't have a friendly atmosphere because you had your first lot of friends there that you'd made from primary school but at college when you get there you immediately see that it's different and you try to sort of fit that environment so you would be classed as a student instead of a child. They think they've reached 16 so then they think, 'I don't have to act immature any more'. I don't know why it happens. I've got a fair idea but I still can't quite put my finger on it. It's a difficult subject!

It was not difficult for interviewees to explain the ways in which college was so different from school; this was summed up for most interviewees by 'more freedom', or, 'They treat you like adults.' '. . . like human beings.' 'You're classed as an adult.' So that, 'At college there's more respect.' As a result, as another Foundation student said: 'Another difference is there's not so many childish people. They take a while to change from school. They start to think "Oh well we're in college now" 'cos they see that they get treated like adults if they act like adults.'

This was symbolized by the first-name terms that nearly all students interviewed (except the engineers at both colleges) were on with their lecturers – 'You don't have to call them "Sir" and "Miss". That shows they're treating you different'; even though, 'after 12 years of calling people "Sir" and "Miss"' it was difficult to change: 'It's a very big shock at first. Weird! Most of my life I've been calling them "Sir" and now he says,

"Call me David!"' The absence of other petty restrictions was also celebrated: 'No uniform but that doesn't really make a big difference.' 'You can sit in class with your coat on or chew gum.' 'You can go out down the town.' 'You get more breaks.' 'So it's completely different, apart from the work.'

This difference was not only because 'The classes here tend to be smaller so they have more time for one-to-one work . . . If they had smaller classes in the school they might make it like that. If they had enough [learning] support teachers to help you in like separate groups in separate rooms but they [the support teachers] tended to come into the classes in school.' 'Small groups is better. You get more attention.' 'In a large class you've got your hand up for about half an hour before the teacher comes to you.' Simply, 'The bigger the group the more hassle you have.' Nor was college different from school merely because of smaller class sizes – down to groups of about ten in college. Learning support lecturers at Foundation level thus had more time and this was particularly appreciated by students who realized, as one said, 'I just needed more time to do things that other kids could just instantly do. I can do other things – like football. I can do that!'

In comparison with school, as the same interviewee continued: 'At college they've got a job to do but they don't just want to just get it over and done with. In school the teachers are all, "Oh I've got this to do. I've got that to do". They've got no time for you.' More time, said another, meant 'They understand the problems better than at school. You get the support you should've got in school because at school they didn't help me understand.'

Interviewees realized this had not necessarily been the fault of their school teachers with whom some quite sympathized: 'I couldn't handle it, teaching up to 30 kids a day, all day every day for five days a week. I'd end up hitting them!' They realized, 'They have to do that 'cos of the way the school is organized.' Especially in some of the schools that Inner City interviewees had attended: 'Like in French lessons all they were doing was controlling the kids and kind of stopping them smashing up the room.' So, 'They couldn't really run the school like college, I suppose because they've got very little kids there as well.' However, as a consequence, 'Even when you're 14 and 15 they're still treating you like a little baby, do you know what I mean? Like telling you what's best and everything. Here they explain things to you. In school they try telling you what to do but here it's different.'

Moreover, there was little choice of what to study in the secondary schools' mainly compulsory National Curriculum: 'Why do you need religious study and all these things?' 'They teach you all stuff you don't need to know.' 'You should have the choice whether you want to do woodwork and CDT. In college you've got much more choice.' But because at school everyone was supposed to be following the same curriculum, 'They were always moaning at me for falling back on a backward level when you're supposed to go forward. Whereas here you do your best and you don't get moaned at.' So at college, 'They don't down-grade you.' Whereas at school, 'They only help the brainy ones', ' . . . the quiet ones.' 'They put me in the lower group because I was dumb. I wasn't dumb really. I didn't get on with them anyway, do you know what I'm saying?'

This selectivity of the school system, in which pupils all followed the same National Curriculum against which they could be graded and compared, was what was resented about the lack of choice at school, along with compulsory attendance and other school rules arising from this. It had been taken for granted by the academically successful students but to those whom it had failed it could be seen to permeate every aspect of their educational experience and to explain the crucial differences between compulsory and post-compulsory learning. For example, the two girls on the Foundation course at Home Counties agreed:

> 'They're very tight on bullying and harassment and that sort of thing at college ...'
> 'It still happens here. It does happen.'
> 'You get a lot of slang for women and not enough for men.'
> 'They're very tight on that as well.'
> 'But I think it's mainly over relationships ... it's more physical in college and it's more verbal at school because I think they know that what they say is going to hurt you more because they say you're stupid or something.'

Freed from this compulsory comparison with others through having made their own decision of what to do in college, even if it was only 'to catch up on what I missed from school', Foundation students reckoned they had changed personally more than any others interviewed, in some cases discovering and developing real talents. This was not only because of the chance to 'lose the label' acquired during their generally unhappy previous experience of compulsory schooling, whether special or mainstream. As one interviewee recalled, he had always got on well with his school teachers 'because they knew that I was a good kid'. But, he went on, 'In college it's different. They teach you to be confident. That's treating you differently.'

'I came as a boy and I shall leave as a man!' joked one. Others, along with their teachers, spoke less ironically of 'becoming my own person'. For perhaps it is in relation to these students more than to any others that the common rhetoric in FE of 'student empowerment' has most meaning. For them empowerment can be linked closely to personal development and not just to the response of colleges to student choices that are often in any case more apparent than real. This applies despite Foundation students' relative lack of qualifications and the fact that the often debilitating nature of their previous psychological, social and sometimes physical circumstances still leaves them generally disadvantaged.

Two young mothers on the Foundation course at Inner City were examples of students at a particular social disadvantage. They had had to grow up very quickly to deal with their situation. As one said:

> When you're younger you have everything done for you. You don't have to do your own cooking and your own washing and all that. You get that done for you and you just sit in front of the television and do nothing. When you have to do everything for yourself it's quite hard ... 'cos reality hits you and you don't know what to do ... It is hard but you know that's life. You have to do it ... it's tiring because I'm doing two things at once, looking after my daughter and going to college. Well, you get stressed out quite a lot.

She was the only student interviewed who admitted to sometimes not eating properly and going hungry (in order to have food for her child), although many others at both colleges said it was 'hard to live' on their allowances and that they were 'struggling'. This was why they worked or sought work; a situation that was appreciated by staff at Inner City College as the prime reason for students not completing courses – 'poverty basically', as one lecturer summed it up. At Home Counties College, travel was the item of expenditure most often mentioned as causing individuals hardship, even though the College was spending £75,000 a year laying on free buses. At Inner City books and equipment were most frequently mentioned.

The other young mother on the Inner City Foundation course had more support from her family, and so 'From 4 o'clock Friday 'til Monday morning I'm out – clubs, parties, dancing and discos. Hackney and all over London . . .' She was thus able to share in the social life enjoyed by the two girls on the Foundation course at Home Counties who spent their weekends dancing and dating, like many of the other young female students interviewed there who confirmed one of their teacher's opinion that: 'Amongst 16- and 17-year-olds there are only two important things in life for 90 per cent of them and that's, one, money and, two, having a good time. Yeah, that is it and that is a product of our culture. That doesn't fit well with what we want, what we want to achieve and what we're trying to achieve and what the government say we must achieve.' For many of the male counterparts of these female students the equivalent attitude was summed up by one Home Counties Foundation student as, 'Football and the pub – that's it: a glorious life!'

Most Foundation students anticipated remaining in college though many would have preferred to find a steady job as an ideal alternative. To them this was an attraction of courses that combined college with work experience where they hoped to find permanent employment. Their aspirations were not generally high in conventional terms and the boys shared with many of the engineering students at levels 2 and 3 the idea of 'doing a good job . . . with my hands'. At Home Counties, like some of the engineers there, some of the boys on the Foundation course were already working weekends and other times with their fathers at painting, landscape-gardening and other manual trades. But, as one 18-year-old Foundation student reflected, looking back on his two years at college, 'In a way college does change you. Probably because you've got your own freedom. You've got your own space as well. And you don't have to be here. You can just say "Fair enough, I'm not going to college" and stay at home.' 'It's down to you,' his friend added.

The belief that individual success or failure is 'down to you' was not a conclusion that students had come to unaided. It had been repeatedly reinforced by their teachers who told them that FE represented a second chance for them to make a fresh start but typically added that to take advantage of it students would have to study and that would be down to them. So, as many interviewees at all three levels of all three pathways said, 'It is up to you.' Thus, 'You have only yourself to blame' for educational failure. The consequences of this widely held belief will next be explored for the Intermediate level students interviewed at the two colleges.

Intermediate

At this level of study the second-chance nature of the provision extends to GCSE resits, plus at Inner City students from abroad whose school qualifications were not recognized in this country. Students are discouraged by the guidance which they receive from retaking the same GCSEs they had failed at school, save the essential English and maths, since results from retakes are not generally good. GCSE resitters and others whose school GCSE grades had been insufficient to enable them to embark immediately upon level 3 courses, typified what one of their teachers called 'the 16-year-old no-hopers'.

Many interviewees blamed their schools or their school-fellows for their poor performance at GCSE and this was the reason they had chosen college in preference to remaining at school. The idea of a 'fresh start' or 'second chance' (like the Foundation students to lose their labels) in a new place away from old ways and old friends was common at both colleges and was a reason that those from outside 'Market Town' gave for wanting to come there (though also, of course, a reason that those staff charged with marketing the college appreciated made local school leavers go elsewhere).

Coming straight from mainstream schooling, if with a gap of one or two years for several of the Inner City interviewees, differences between school and college were again salient for these students and as above centred on the notion of 'freedom' as opposed to compulsory attendance with its accompanying regulations. Interviewees accepted their own responsibility for success or failure in this new situation. For example, this 16-year-old Home Counties girl:

> I was supposed to be staying on [at school] but when I got my exam results I was very disappointed 'cos I only got one C and I found out I couldn't resit my exams at school. I was in a bit of trouble and I didn't know what to do because the school did not tell me anything what to do if I didn't get the grades I wanted. I didn't revise enough for my exams. I was very surprised with my maths grade; I got a C but I wasn't spending enough time revising. It was my fault. I just wasn't motivated. I was just so bored, sitting there reading the same stuff over and over again. Boring! But I'm still not motivated. I just can't be bothered to do the work. I suppose at school you're always pushed to do the work but at college you're just left to get on and do it. So you don't get on and do it! I sometimes need a very big push to get me started and then I will do it. It's just actually getting me started on it . . . My friends at school are still getting treated more or less the same as when they were at school, still getting detentions and things and it's a bit stupid really. I suppose at college it's the feeling that you're treated as an adult not a child and you're allowed your own responsibilities and if you like you have to have your own motivation. That is a problem for me but in general you do your thing.

It is such contradictory demands – wanting independence while still needing a push – that have to be mediated by teachers seeking to motivate students to stay on course and gain their target qualifications.

In Inner City with traditionally low post-16 participation rates in the borough, what evidence there is suggests that there are at least as many 16–18-year-olds in the locality outside the system as there are in school and college or on training schemes. Indeed, many interviewees compared themselves to those they knew who 'lay in bed all day' or 'stayed at home doing nothing – literally nothing' by contrast to those in college who were 'trying to better themselves' and had 'ambition'. It was noticeable that, as well as the perennial discussion in sociology classes, even at this GCSE level, of whether or not 'education makes you middle class', students used participation in further education as signalling those with 'ambition', 'to get a foot on the ladder', 'make it', 'better themselves' and 'be somebody'. For instance, one 17-year-old black GCSE student at Inner City College stated, 'I would like to think of myself as middle class but I know I'm not but maybe [I think like that] because, like, I'm trying to be.' While her classmate asked, 'What future can you build together if your boyfriend ain't got no ambition, do you know what I mean? It's all right [if] he's not working but he's at college. He's doing something, not just sitting around. But if he's got no ambition and don't want a job or something like that, he's no good to you, is he?' So she concluded, 'The difference could be between the people who are in college and who are out', rather than significant differences between groups of students within the College. In Home Counties, with the highest staying-on rate anywhere in the South East, 'Unless you're an outcast, it seems like strange if you don't go on to further education.'

At intermediate and also advanced levels therefore, students at both places looked on everyone in their college as the same:

> I think we all look at each other as one class, rather than look at him as 'Oh he's a higher class, or he's a lower class – he ain't got the same shoes on as everyone else'. No, we look at everyone as equal. (Inner City)

> 'Cos you don't know the potential that person has got. Someone at A-level can't say that somebody at GCSE hasn't got the same potential as them. You can look down on them but in reality you don't know what their potential is . . . You see, when you're a student, you might take a cleaning job just to get by 'cos you're not going to stay there for ever. It's just to help you get by. (Inner City)

> It's difficult for this kind of college . . . but compared with secondary school – they were definitely sorting people out [there]. It was blatantly obvious that middle-class kids got more opportunity to go up a grade and all the working-class people were in the bottom groups. It was definitely so obvious just because they misbehaved or whatever they'd all get sort of ripped off and they all came from the same sort of background. Whereas here it's not so obvious because you've got so many different cultures – people from Hong Kong and different people – and mature students together with kids coming out of school and you've got people from all different districts, from as far away as 15 miles and 25 miles, people from 'Big Town' nearby. It's quite a mixture. You do get sort of different groups of people in the canteen and that. You get sort of the grungey people, who seem to be dying out now. You get the sort of more hippified people with dreadlocks and whatever. A lot of that is to do with fashion . . . But I think at college they do pretty well to keep people together. In my group there's a lot of older people and some

of them are more middle than working class but as they're all lumped in together I can't really see if the college is sort of channelling them in all sort of different directions. I can't see it happening here. I can't see a class thing coming up. (Home Counties)

However, two Home Counties College A-level sociology students thought that parental background played a large part in influencing who completed courses to what level. One commented: 'Well, you don't want to sound superior but, I think if I'd have dropped out of college or just dropped one of my A-levels then my mum and dad would've been very disappointed because you're not the sort of person to give up and you'll regret it in future years.' Her friend added, 'I feel so guilty towards my parents, not because they're pressuring me but because I want them to be proud of me.' They continued:

I know what you mean because you think about in what class are people socialized into this proudness and you kind-of think that working-class parents kind-of just let kids get on with it and aren't one hundred per cent interested. I mean, I hate the fact that I'm saying this.

No, I know what you mean because I've talked to people who have dropped out and I asked them, 'Oh, what do your parents say about this?' and they go, 'Oh, they're not bothered'" and, I mean, there have been times in my A-level courses when I've thought, 'Oh, I really want to drop this subject', but it would be so much easier to do that if you thought, 'I'm going to go home tonight and my parents aren't going to care', but you know that if I drop this A-level my parents are going to go mad and I think that is the very big factor that stops you doing it.

In comparison, from her own experience of the conflicting influence of peers in compulsory secondary schooling in Inner City borough, one of the adult AAT students recalled:

It was all right for the first three to four years [at secondary school]. I was always one of those really quiet children. I was classed as one of the mature ones which I found really boring – too sensible to do anything but actually I didn't feel confident to do anything. I was always a loner but then I got in with a group of people and you come to be accepted and you're doing things as a group . . . and so I got in with this crowd and I think it was just getting out and being more independent and we used to go out a lot and it was a lot more interesting than school work. In fact, it was brilliant! The usual story.

There was some evidence from some of the interviewees, as well as from the complaints of their teachers about them (as above p. 00), that college was experienced in the same way by some students as the interviewee above remembered her last years at school. This was particularly the case with GCSE resitters, for example those young women who admitted to going into Market Town at lunchtime and sometimes not returning from the pub in the afternoon, or the young man who came to Inner City College 'for something to do' rather than be unemployed, and 'to meet people', and 'because there's so many nice-looking girls here'. Or, as another young man there said, 'Well really, to be truthful, it's the girls. In college there's so many girls it's just enjoyable being in the college, just looking at them!' This was also a reason for coming to a bigger rather than a smaller college: 'There's more people to meet.'

Certainly, both colleges have to encourage their students to balance their social lives with their study, as well as nowadays for many of them with part-time work. It is a delicate tight-rope to walk: 'Not pushing you so hard. They can overdo it. Like at school. But they won't let you drop the course work. They'll get it out of you.' What works in one college with one group of students has to be presented differently with another – what were openly called 'attendance checks' at Home Counties as compared with systems of 'student support' at Inner City. Similarly, tutors have to deal differently with very different individuals, including the mature students, to whose presence in classes one young student interviewee attributed the more respectful way college as opposed to school teachers treated their students.

The tutorial system at both colleges worked best in sustaining students who were on full-time courses when the tutor was also one of their subject teachers, as with all the Foundation and engineering courses and some on A-level sociology. If they were not also the teacher of one of their subjects, their tutors had been most useful to the A-level students in helping them apply to higher education. For the GCSE students, tutorials were also generally accepted as 'useful' if the tutor was also their teacher – 'Then if we haven't been in, he gives us the worksheets.' If not: 'We just go in there, do the things we've got to do and go out. The Thursday one is just a waste of time. We just put our attendance on and just go and we might as well do that on Tuesday. The Tuesday one is OK sometimes. We have like discussions and they ask you how you're getting on and what you're doing, just discussing with the tutor.'

For these Intermediate-level students, smaller college classes compensated for less time than they had been accustomed to spending on two-year GCSE courses at school as compared with one-year college courses reduced to fit 21 or 16 hours. In itself this meant 'It's a lot more left up to you than they do at school 'cos you don't have so much time in the class for a start.' If classes became too small however, as many did with rapid decay from promising starts in the first term, the remaining students and their teachers became disheartened, especially if classes then merged and 'if the people come back the teacher has to go over everything again and you can't keep on doing that'.

For some students, like the two following students from girls' schools in Inner City College, the level of tutorial support and the smaller size of classes was not enough to make up for the order that they missed in their schools: 'I think it would be better [in school sixth form than college] because there would be more people of my own age. I think they would treat you better there, look after you more.' So, '. . .in some ways I miss school. I miss sort of having the lunch times and the break times and all that stuff. I miss some of the people . . .' Interviewees supported the idea that FE appealed to those who were 'more mature' or 'ready for it'. 'It's hard to say if most people are ready. It depends on where they've come from – what their family situation is and the school they've been to – but most people seem ready enough but you get a few who are uneasy and might go back to school but the drift is more from school to college.' There is no systematic tracking of these movements either locally or nationally.

There was more of a sense of community at school, and college was widely regarded as more impersonal, largely because it was so much bigger. As we have noted, a college has to work hard to create a corporate life with which students want to identify (see further below). The isolation of one subject from another that we have seen teachers complain about as they struggle to deliver cut-down courses in an ever-more-intensive college day makes this task increasingly difficult. It becomes another of the conflicting demands staff have to juggle.

The many demands that students make upon the colleges have to be balanced in the crucial 'image' that the institution projects to potential students. Creating an attractive environment and effective marketing is a major priority to which considerable resources are devoted. To help with this, at both colleges the students' union (previously a fairly nominal body) was supported and financed by senior management to organize entertainment and sporting events. As the President of Home Counties students' union astutely remarked: 'We are aware of how much they need to get customers and we can use that to our advantage. I mean, each year we're getting more and more students enrolling in the College and that's good for the SU too, for organizing social activities and things. So the College backs up the SU and we back up the College because what is good for us is good for them.' The students' union could use the Students' Charter to build up its role and, indeed, the Home Counties President was the only student interviewee who mentioned the government's 'Charter for Further Education'.

Being new and shiny, Home Counties College had an advantage in attracting students in comparison with older, rival colleges. Market Town was clearly preferred as 'a nice place' by students from other 'rougher' towns, as they described them, where they could have gone to college. The hierarchy of competing schools and colleges locally relates to a similar rank ordering of higher education institutions. The academic sixth-form college in nearby Big Town, together with some school sixth forms and the private schools aimed at the 'Ivy League' of traditional universities. Most of the Home Counties students who intended to enter HE aimed instead for universities of the second rank, the sixth-form college having creamed those trying for Oxbridge entrance. At Inner City College in comparison, many interviewees hoping to enter HE had applied to local former polytechnics.

For its part, slogans such as 'Inner City is a happening college' were not as vacuous as they might appear but contributed towards impressing potential students, along with the video of the College fashion show that appealed to school students, whether boys or girls but for different reasons. Several black interviewees stressed the attraction to them of 'a black college', as they described Inner City, and the College built upon the positive aspects of this image with events such as the Black Awareness Week that the black interviewees who mentioned it certainly appreciated. At the same time, despite these rival attractions and subsidized college transport (above), the ending of travel grants is restricting access to all but local colleges, just as in HE many students are nowadays saving on costs by studying locally whilst remaining at home, as was the intention of the Inner City interviewees reported above.

However, choices of college were also influenced by what has become the normalization of remaining in post-compulsory education which itself exerts peer pressure on young people. Many of the level 2 engineering students on their one-year course at Home Counties appeared to have confirmed their choice of going to college early in their last year at school and 'stopped worrying about it', as one said, thereafter. Partly, as with other students, this was 'what everyone does nowadays' and this normalization foreclosed other possibilities such as Modern Apprenticeships. Even though these were lads who might previously have gone straight into work and for whom a work-based route to qualification was stated by them to be a preferred alternative, they did not know about Modern Apprenticeships and other schemes on which they could have pursued such an option. This was despite the fact that there were agents managing schemes in engineering in both localities. A local careers officer related this to the way the College 'zapped' the schools early through its 'Year 9 and 10 Initiative' to 'clean up quickly', compared to which applying anywhere else – through managing agents for Jobskills schemes, for instance – was much more effort.

From the students' point of view, they appreciated suddenly being in demand, even from school teachers with whom they might not have been particularly popular previously: 'It was like "Come to the sixth form" and all of a sudden they were being friendly to you.' Another student commented: 'When I said I was coming back in September they were like delighted. Could it be to do with money? I don't know. They looked on me supposedly as an adult, not a kid in uniform any more.' As for college: 'Well, the college is like a business and they try to teach us as best they can, to try to provide the best service as they can, and as we enrol we're worth money to them, so they teach us and if we don't come up to scratch, or if we like start pissing around, or not have enough attendance, they would lose the money. But it's basically up to you to keep your attendance up.'

Consequently most student interviewees confirmed the supposition of a Home Counties Assistant Principal that 'All students have a good idea how much they are worth – between £1,500 to £3,000 . . .' Indeed, often they had been told this by their teachers, so that, as he continued, 'everybody is pretty clear that they are valuable commodities as far as the initial competitiveness is concerned'. In the view of some teachers this made for 'arrogant students' who were reluctant to accept guidance and who held out for courses beyond their capabilities. Students themselves certainly did not appreciate that their work is broken up and individually funded. Nor had most of them been in college long enough to make comparisons over time to estimate whether the market in education had improved the quality of their experience. The previously poor reputation of Inner City College had put off a number of – especially older – students from wanting to attend it. However, all those interviewed who declared such an initial reluctance also said that their presuppositions had been unjustified and that they, like the large majority of students responding to the College's own 'Student Satisfaction Survey', would now recommend the College to a friend.

All of the Intermediate-level students interviewed at Inner City intended to remain in further education, most of them at that College. Their aspirations were high – one 16-year-old alternating between the attractions of going to the United States to become a basketball star and remaining in Inner City to go on to the A-levels needed to be a doctor. Lawyer, journalist and nurse were among other aspirations that these GCSE sociologists mentioned. Again, it was a delicate balancing act for tutors and subject teachers to, on the one hand, maintain students' motivation and, on the other, to get them to be realistic.

It is a dilemma familiar to careers' advisers and indeed, college careers officers seconded from the local Careers Service played a large part in student decision-making at this level. For example:

> Well, I talked to the careers people about what I should be doing next year and what I could do, so I could come back here and do a GNVQ or maybe an A/S level or I could try and find some work or work part-time and come to college but I haven't decided at the moment. I spoke to my parents about it and they said I should come back to college but I think my time would be better spent if I could get a job.

While another young man at Home Counties who was already in a job and attended college part-time appreciated at first hand the importance of qualifications that was emphasized as essential by so many interviewees at all levels of study:

> I feel I've got to get some qualifications behind me so as not to get stuck in a rut because I can see myself slipping into staying in my job for years and years because I work with people who've been in the same job for, you know, ten years and they get stuck in a rut. They're not thick or anything. They just ended up getting a full-time job without the opportunity to get back into education and it's very difficult to live on the wage. I mean, obviously I'm living with my parents but if you haven't got the advantage of that it's very difficult.

Some GCSE retakers had evidently been somewhat disoriented by their failure to gain the grades they had expected. This was reflected by two girls at Home Counties College whose parents were professors and teachers respectively:

> I don't know. I had an idea last year, you know, but I was going to do communications A-level but as I'm taking communications studies at GCSE that's put me off it but I want to do photography; I really enjoy that. I like doing arty subjects because they're not really that academic. I don't think of art college. I wanted to go to university but I don't know, I'll have to see what happens now. I have to just take it day by day.

> Well, I want to do my English and my other GCSEs, do my A-levels and then I want to go to Australia . . . and then I'll come back to go to university to do law or an English degree. I'm not sure.

This uncertainty and vagueness was not confined to those whose plans had been upset however. To quote again the Home Counties SU President, herself an A-level student:

> A lot of people are very unsure. They're in education because it's sort of the done thing and they aren't able to get a job. So I think quite a lot of people are studying because there's nothing else to do. Time passes them by because they're not really sure what they want to do – if they want to go to university or if they want

to get jobs. I think it's just because it's the norm to go and do your A-levels and go to university, that's what everybody does. There's only a few who actually know what they want to do. I would say it has become the norm to go to college over the last five years. That's a change . . . Higher education not so much but further education – it's very: 'Why aren't you studying at college or school or whatever?' I think if the economy picked up a lot of school-leavers would go straight for jobs, especially the ones who don't have a clue where they're going.

Most GCSE students hoped to go on to A-levels, while for engineers their one-year BTEC Firsts would lead on to two-year Nationals, just as one-year AAT Foundation led on to their two-year Intermediate NVQ course. Students were not very conscious of the curricular changes that we have seen had impinged so strongly upon their teachers. These differences can best be examined in the next section dealing with students at NCVQ level 3 whether in A-level sociology classroom, BTEC National engineering workshop, or on work-based AAT.

Advanced

At this level the students whose experience of further education was most similar to their previous schooling were the A-level sociologists interviewed at both colleges. It would also be the most similar to their higher education experience that they anticipated. As one said, going to college rather than remaining in school sixth form was 'a trial run for going to university'. Because of this continuity and because they were doing what was expected of them, they questioned their experience least. Indeed, their classroom-based mode of study had continued unchanged save that it is at a higher level, so that the demands upon them in FE were those of traditional A-level in comparison with their previous GCSEs in most cases. They were thus sixth-formers in further education for whom FE represented an alternative to sixth form. Also because their further education built upon their previous largely successful school experience, often supported by families who, if not professionally qualified as many of their parents were in Home Counties, were in Inner City members of the churches that have been shown to play a significant part in black educational achievement.

The newer GNVQ represented an alternative route to higher education for those who did not have the requisite GCSE grades to follow the A-level path. This GNVQ path forms the second level of a tripartite tertiarism (or tertiary modern schooling) emerging in schools and colleges. A number of teachers worried that an advanced GNVQ would not meet higher education requirements of students taking these courses as an alternative route to HE. Indeed, some students, at the same time as they were declaring all students to be equal, also distinguished between what they called 'A-level people' and 'GNVQ people'. Their attitudes are indicated by two Inner City A-level sociologists in conversation:

'A lot of people who drop out of A-level tend to do GNVQ. It could be they just don't have the intellect to do A-levels. There's no way it's equivalent to A-level.'
'It's degrading A-level if they use that as a way to get into higher education because we're working so hard to get our "A"-levels and they're just coming

along and everyone is passing [GNVQ]. Some universities don't recognize them 'cos they tell you, like at school and things, "Oh you can do BTEC and GNVQ and still get into uni", but I'm thinking then why do they still have A-level?'

'Like in biology, we had quite a few to start off with and this year you didn't see any of them.'

'Everyone has lame excuses like, "Oh it's too hard" or "I don't like the teacher".'

'I think some of them were on the wrong course.'

'Like what's-her-name, wasn't it? They were saying you have to get A-level to get into uni and she didn't want to do A-levels at all.'

'I could tell she was not an A-level student. I mean, some people you can see whether – I couldn't say they weren't good enough – but whether they are capable of taking up an A-level subject or not.'

'You can tell – the time they turn up to lessons, how often they come in and participate in class.'

'Now that girl's doing GNVQ. I used to see her all the time frumpy and now she's happy. Now she even talks about the work she's done. She's extremely proud of her work.'

'She used to be very grumpy.'

'She used to stand outside smoking . . . [But now] She's, like, mega, mega happy.'

None of the students we interviewed who were taking GNVQs could be described as 'mega, mega happy' but they were not discontented either. They and their teachers proclaimed that GNVQ was just as demanding as A-level, or more so, and indeed some of the A-level interviewees – though not the two above – appreciated that this could be the case. In fact, GNVQ was not experienced as so radically different from traditional forms of study like A-level. This could be seen in that GNVQ students also relied upon textbooks, teachers' notes and class handouts for much of their information, even though they were supposed to actively 'discover' this information for themselves. Indeed, A-level students were also constantly exhorted to 'work by themselves' on their own initiative but also welcomed didactic teaching and explicit direction for what would be expected of them in examination for which practice papers developed their 'technique'. However, modular A-levels, which were being introduced at both colleges but which were not taken by any of our interviewees, moved away from this terminal written examination towards assessment of assignments, if not the continual assessment of competence on demand which was the original model for GNVQ.

The BTEC phase tests, which were similar to and pre-dated GNVQ assessments, were accepted by the engineering students as part of the course. They were expected of them so they did them and they could retake them after a period of revision and preparation if they were unsuccessful at first. The same applied to the NVQ practical assessments for the accountancy technicians, which these classes also undertook periodically together – and not on individual demand or at work (which was impractical), even though this might have been originally intended by NCVQ. In the absence of opportunities for accrediting competences at work, AAT students were even more heavily reliant upon their single textbook for the course than either A-level, GNVQ or BTEC students at this level.

Engineering at both colleges and at both levels 2 and 3 (BTEC 1st and National) was vocationally oriented by definition. It was a full-time (16 hours a week) course, equivalent, like one GNVQ3, to two A-levels. This and the isolation of the engineering section within the colleges contributed to a shared vocational culture amongst the students, especially after two or three years of study. Several of the fathers of interviewees at Home Counties College worked in, or in a couple of cases owned, small engineering companies locally. Their sons had a realistic appreciation of their job prospects (as confirmed by the College careers adviser) and did not intend to continue in education beyond level 3. In this respect they exhibited what Professor Smithers has called the 'discouragement effect' of progressing to HE that was shared by other interviewees, particularly mature students if working full-time, but also by younger students who did not relish the prospect of graduating without work and in debt in three or four years' time. They felt that they would have had 'enough' of education by the time they left at 18. For example:

> I don't want to stay on for a third year seeing the same old faces every day. I like it but it's a bit much sometimes. But I might stay on if I can't find another job. I don't want to go to college or university. I wouldn't be able to cope with it. A friend of my mine goes and she's taken a loan out. Before you know it you've got a debt over your head that you're going to be paying for the rest of your life.

These students were unlike most engineers interviewed in Inner City College, many of whom came from Third World countries and included several asylum-seekers. There was in any case no engineering industry locally for them to have any contact with and their notions of employment prospects for engineers were hazy at best. For example, one East African refugee said he would like to be an air traffic controller but had no idea how to achieve such a goal and had in fact only thought of it through casual conversation with a lecturer just prior to interview. These students therefore postponed a decision by hoping to enter HE. Whether their English and maths in particular would qualify them to do so, or whether if it did they would satisfactorily complete HND or degree courses at the local former polytechnics they considered applying to, was doubted by their lecturers.

Similar reservations about whether the basic English and maths 'core' (now 'key') 'skills' of engineering students were sufficient to pass all of the BTEC phase tests necessary for full qualification were registered by their lecturers at the Home Counties College. Partly this reflected the school achievement of the students which averaged only two or three GCSEs at A-C in most cases. In contrast with this modest achievement in the academic National Curriculum at school, many engineering students spoke warmly of the pleasures of making things and getting their hands dirty at work and in college. Despite the fact that tutors at both colleges arranged extra 'core skills' support for these students, either by coaching them themselves and/or arranging for them to go to the Learning Support Centre, students often did not take full advantage of these affordances to learning. This was because, first, there was some stigma attached to doing so and, second, this was additional to the normal demands upon them and cut into what they regarded as their free time and/or time when they were working if they had jobs.

Many more of these older and more qualified students had part-time jobs. In fact, there was a hierarchy of part-time employment evident amongst interviewees as between A-level students, especially at Inner City College, who could least afford time off from heavy timetables of study but who were working the longest hours – up to 18 hours a week in some cases, and younger GCSE students who found it harder to find part-time work. This was not only because they were younger and so lacked qualifications and experience but also because, especially at Home Counties, more advantaged family backgrounds made many A-level students more attractive to employers. They thus worked, not only in pubs and waitressing but in boutiques and art galleries. Even for them though, the pressures of this part-time work ate into the time that they needed to study for three A-levels – really a full-time occupation in itself. Indeed, the pressures of and necessity for part-time work are widely acknowledged as contributing to lack of progression in further education.

If they aimed for higher education students deferred vocational decision and extended their 'planning horizon' by another three or four years before they intended to enter the full-time labour market. Thus A-level students who had entered college with very definite vocational intentions that they had held for some time during school (to be a probation officer, for example), found themselves undecided after two years deconstructing society in sociology. Another example of students changing their vocational aspirations due to their further education experience was students combining A-level sociology with music who had come to realize through comparison with other students at the music centre in Home Counties College that they might not after all become professional musicians, as perhaps they had believed and been encouraged in previously by their parents and schools. Instead, they thought now of merely 'writing about music', thus joining the legion of would-be journalists in F&HE and the majority choice of occupation of all A-level sociology students interviewed at both colleges.

While many students at all levels expressed an interest in their studies and said that they enjoyed them, and while they might have changed some of their opinions and intentions partly as a reaction to their courses of study (as above and also the Foundation students), it was only mature students who declared that their subject of study itself had had any profound effect upon their lives and how they now saw the world. For example, a 39-year-old mother of four who described herself as 'Happily divorced for the past year' and for whom, typically of HE access students, 'Coming back to education was one of the reasons for divorce', enjoyed her three A-levels so much: 'I don't want to go home of an evening . . . It's definitely changed my way of thinking. I mean, I used to go home and watch television and I don't even have my television on now. I just sit there with my books.' Typically again, she added:

> I've dropped a lot of old friends since coming to college . . . because they're all
> mothers with kids and their life revolves around their families and husbands and
> my life doesn't revolve around that any more . . . especially Turkish women, I
> don't see hardly any Turkish women now because I've done the un-done thing,
> I've left my husband . . . A lot of my old friends, they wouldn't understand my

new friends, they say, 'Oh you're a college bum now and a boffin' . . . Before I was just a mother. Now I'm a mum and I'm me.

This case again exemplifies the second-chance nature of so much further education provision, but even for those younger students moving predictably from the good school GCSE grades that qualified them for two years' A-level study as the preparation for HE at 18-plus, their conventional subject choices in the humanities broadened their education in a traditional, humanistic sense. For example, as expressed by an A-level theatre studies, sociology and English literature student: 'it makes you question a lot more things, more than you've ever done at school because the teachers make you question things, whereas at school they just say, "This is right" and "This is right". Here they're constantly saying, "Maybe that isn't right" and "Maybe this isn't right" and it helps you have a wider view on things that way.' This contributed especially to the ethos of Home Counties College where up to half the student body follow such courses.

The work-based course for accountancy technicians was notable at both colleges for having least 'spill-over' effect on other areas of students' lives, largely perhaps because it occupied only one day a week in their busy lives already taken up with family and other commitments. These effects included how they thought about things outside their technical concerns at work – not that these concerns necessarily coincided with what they were taught in college but this is a common misalignment in traditional day release to college-based courses. It was not overcome by the NVQ assessment of what were supposedly work-based competences. For in this respect, the AAT course was representative of training for occupations where the contents of a standards-based qualification far outstrip what is actually required in the workplace.

One thing shared by all interviewees at all levels of study, save the minority who might once have progressed via sixth form to HE, was that 30 years ago most of them would not have been in any sort of post-compulsory education at all. This was obvious to many students, including the 16-year-old resitting her GCSEs at Inner City College who said that one indication of how life was getting worse in the country at present was: 'because you have to work harder and harder to get a worse and worse job. You have to go to university to get what 30 years ago you didn't even have to have A-levels for.'

Even in the case of the older accountancy students, their study was to gain qualifications that would either advance or secure their positions if they were in employment – as most were at Home Counties; or, if they were not – as in most cases at Inner City – would they hoped help them to gain or regain employment. From their perspective also:

Experience alone is not enough nowadays. You've got to have qualifications as well. Employers are demanding that. So with these kids all coming out with six, seven and eight GCSEs – well, I think they're easier than what they were before – but you haven't got anything to compete with them, although your experience is better, so you've got to increase what qualifications you've got just to be on some sort of par with them.

Yet some interviewees welcomed the brave new world of lifetime learning. A world in which it is now necessary for the majority of the future workforce to remain for as long as possible in institutionalized education and training, with periodic returns to learning thereafter, as they pursue a variety of occupations throughout their working lives. Rather than being sentenced to a secure job for life, this could be welcomed as quite an inviting prospect for a young and energetic person, particularly as learning and earning might also be interspersed with leisure and travel. For example, another two Home Counties A-level sociologists (other than the two whose views on the importance of parental support were reported above) answered the classic question 'Where do you see yourself in five years?' with:

> 'Travelling around.'
> 'Bumming off the state for a while.'
> 'Apart from like nurse things when you're really small, I've never for a long time had any idea about a set career or anything like that.'
> 'Before I came here I was going to be an osteopath. That was my whole career destiny and now it's, sort of, do sociology and see what happens.'
> 'She really was definite about what she was going to do.'
> 'But now I just think there's so much more out there that I can do.'

Of course, it requires some self-confidence supported by the assurance of material and parental support to entertain such prospects. Very few of the Inner City interviewees talked in such a manner – though there was one, perhaps exceptional, member of the Foundation course there who claimed to be travelling around the world from his home in St Helena and who foresaw moving on from London to Africa and elsewhere. But other students were already, as it were, pioneering a lifestyle of moving from education to part-time work, saving only to go skiing abroad, or to travel in Europe in the summer holidays, having placed what has been called 'a moratorium' on any sense of direction or incremental progression.

For example, one of the few men on the AAT course at Home Counties College recalled how after leaving a previous college:

> I sort of did nothing for a while. Well, I was working part-time while I was studying, doing bar work, and I went on working in a pub and then eventually got a job where I am now, three or months ago now. I'm a trainee accountant. It just sort of happened that I went in for accountancy. I didn't want to go to work at all. I was quite happy. I was working in a pub and I was getting enough money that I could go out whenever I wanted to even though I was only working part-time pretty much but being down the pub I used to stay down there all night sort of thing. They used to close the bar and sit down and have a few drinks, leave about three o'clock in the morning, go home and don't get up 'til the afternoon and go through the same routine. I was quite happy with that. My parents, on the other hand, weren't and they wanted me to get a job and they used to go on and on about 'Get a job, get a job!'

So that, eventually and under parental pressure, like the young woman who asserted simply that 'If I don't start working in college my mum says she's going to kick me out of the house', this interviewee had gained full-time employment from which he was now seconded to college.

The above might be regarded as just a phase that the young man went through, yet part of our argument is that such phases are being extended for more and more people. Many youngsters have periods of education and training in which they move from one scheme or course to another without ever entering full-time, secure employment. This pattern of life is reaching steadily up the age range to include wider social groups beyond those for whom it has for long been habitual. Even in the inner city, it is not unusual for young people to intersperse periodic education and training with periods of casual work and/or travel, especially to relatives abroad.

As employment – particularly the prospect of one occupation for the whole of a working life – becomes increasingly less relevant for defining social identities so consumer and leisure identities become more important. There is a contradiction of course that conventional consumer and leisure identities are harder to sustain without regular income and this partly accounts for the proliferation of counter-cultures amongst the young. Despite the relentless vocational pressures for conformity to which education at all levels now subjects students, alternative youth cultures generally oppose the whole work ethic, or 'Dogma of Work', which derives identity from occupation.

As we say, many interviewees could welcome a move away from dependence upon work – especially the prospect of just one job for their whole life – until they reflected that, without parental or other support, they would require some other source of income to sustain them in the periods between moving from one different job to another. Such a reflection gave pause to even the most confident and assured. While we have already seen that to those who lacked the personal resources – material and educational – to entertain it, this prospect of enterprising and varied forms of contracted and self-employment did not appeal at all. They sought instead the security of 'a steady job' in which they could 'keep their heads down' and 'hang on' if not 'get on'. We have also mentioned that the motivation to acquire qualifications for those released to FE from full-time work was often precisely to hang on to that employment faced with possible redundancy and the use their employers made of new technology.

The value of further education is changing for the new and emerging lifestyles in a future in which earning, learning and leisure may be mixed together in new combinations. FE not only has vocational relevance in preparing and reskilling students for such employment as might be available to them, as well as updating them to use the latest technologies – as in the GNVQ IT course reported on by the teacher in the previous chapter. Increasingly also, FE imparts the generalized knowledge that employers now say they require of a workforce able to adapt flexibly to a variety of changing demands and not trained to perform only particular limited operations. Such generalized knowledge could also give a greater critical understanding of society as a whole and it has been seen in the last chapter that many teachers are dedicated to educating their students in such a spirit. Many of them oppose the restriction of study to vocational levels of competence and seek to make connections between increasingly isolated and disconnected programmes of study.

No matter how much things change, however, for those experiencing them for the first time they appear normal. As one teacher speculated, most students were not in a position to notice the deterioration which she alleged in the quality of their learning because: 'It's a kind of norm. They've come up through the whole school system where things have been squeezed all the way through.' Unlike their teachers, if they have been employed for a while, students entering FE for the first time, whether straight from school or later in life, lack the perspective on which to take a comparative view of before and after. They did not know, for example, to what extent in the replacement of the one-time TEC General and Communications Studies units by GNVQ Communications key skills, lists of tasks to be performed in specified settings to generate certain evidence had been substituted for attempts to teach general economic and political literacy through project work in set syllabuses. They could not therefore estimate very easily the quality of their learning in comparison with what it might have been like previously, especially as most new entrants to FE were the first in their families to continue with education after school.

Yet at Inner City two or three mature students had either been employed by the College for some time or had attended some years previously and they attributed the complete transformation and improvement they saw in conditions as primarily due to the new security system and then to the personal influence of the new Principal who had had it installed. Two AAT students' reflections went further however:

'It's a massive change, really massive. Definitely the student being the client, it's much more student-orientated, much more to do with helping students. If a student had a tantrum in the old days he got booted out. Nowadays it's "Find out what's causing the trouble. Solve it. Do something about it."'

'It's not only that is it? Isn't it the amount of money they receive as well?'

'By the fact that we're funded per result. So you want to help the student actually achieve something . . . The teachers have changed massively as well . . . Do you remember the guy with the grey hair?'

'Oh yes!'

'By the time they found out he was having a nervous breakdown and got rid of him . . .'

'But they knew that the year before. They didn't do anything about it. That would never happen now. They would do something about it straight away. I think that's the money factor because otherwise the whole class fails. Then they lose all their funding because if they lose their funding then the Principal will start saying "Is it worth having that course in the college?" That's her attitude and then their job is gone . . . [Whereas before] If you filled your class up you got paid. It didn't matter if the teacher wasn't very good . . . It's definitely much better. One thing they're very keen on here, dealing with clients, actually treating people in a proper manner. I think they do that well. The attitude when I came in, when I arrived, and I was quite horrified at it, but it was a standard attitude: "I'm an accountant. I'm a book-keeper. I shouldn't have to put up with that" – and that was to the student! So the student was considered something really foreign, you know, that decent people didn't really have to put up with. That was five years ago. Now everybody is open to the fact that these students really need help. They haven't had much of a chance before and the College is going to do everything in its power to help them . . . [and] the funding has helped to concentrate upon them. I mean, they've set up all sorts of support for them, like you've got lots of students with language difficulties and they get special classes and there's always signs up everywhere saying "Are you having problems with maths? You are not alone. Come and see us". That wasn't there before, or if it was you wouldn't get much help with it. This has always been a special needs college anyway. We've always been good in that area but now we've developed that to the general population. We've realized that the general population have special needs.'

Such a view is anecdotal but indicative of the opinions of two non-teaching staff of the College as well as those of students unusually able to make a comparison in changes over time. It is in obvious contrast to the opinions of many of the teachers quoted in Chapter 4 and would appear to endorse the view of management reflected in Chapter 3. In our final chapter we attempt to reconcile these apparently contradictory perspectives preliminary to drawing from their synthesis a conclusion as to the future of further education.

Chapter 6

Mass further education

> . . . no longer will I follow you oblique-like through the inspired form of the third person singular and the moods and hesitensies of the deponent but address myself to you, with the empirative of my vendettative, provocative and out direct . . .
>
> James Joyce, *Finnegan's Wake* (with acknowledgements to Mike Cooley)

The quality of further education

It seemed at first impossible to us to reconcile two such opposed views as those of the two students quoted at the end of the previous chapter and their teachers reported at the end of Chapter 4. The latter remained sceptical or resistant, while the former tended to support the more optimistic views of the managers quoted in Chapter 3. They might have been describing two different institutions instead of offering perceptions of the same college. Moreover, the limited time available to us and the qualitative approach that we had adopted precluded any attempt to quantify by comparative measurement of before and after which version of reality was 'correct'. Such measures as were available – improvement in examination results and the increase in numbers of students – indicated that the quality of the further education provided had indeed improved. There were too other real gains in the new facilities available to students and in the more equal and individual treatment both colleges declared it was now their mission to extend to the communities they served.

However, the quality of experience is by definition unquantifiable, as the Principal of Home Counties College explained in a long discussion of the quality of further education:

> It depends on what you mean by quality . . . Where do you put the time of a tutor to stay behind after the class has finished to deal with a particular student who has a particular problem about doing their homework because they haven't got the resources at home, or whatever it is, and that tutor being not able to do that sort of thing? And if it takes place or doesn't take place is there a qualitative difference to what you're offering within the organization?

The intractable nature of these questions was illustrated, he said, by the debate which had occurred in the College about reducing the amount of teaching time for A-levels. Two years previously this had been cut to only four and a half taught hours a week for a two-year course despite the objections of teachers. These objections were not assuaged by the fact that exam results actually improved slightly because many teachers still argued that quality was lost due to the loss of time to talk around the subject and to take a broader and more critical view by making connections with other areas of student experience and study.

Discussion of quality relates to that of 'standards', the maintenance of which we have seen was vital to staff self-esteem. For teachers of academic subjects this related, as above, to traditional humanist notions of educating the whole person by making students critically aware as well as by enabling them to master bodies of specialist subject knowledge. Upholding standards in vocational courses was, we also heard from our interviewees, related to trade practices and often to teachers' expectations of good practice derived from their own experiences in the trade. That new types of student would require more help and support to reach these same standards was regarded as a further professional demand often needing a response from new professional specialists – in key skills support, English-language teaching or learning support.

The debate about quality is therefore, as the Principal continued, 'horrendously difficult', not only because 'we're confused about what we mean by quality', but also because 'what we've always resisted as a profession – and this is deep in our values – is simple measurement by outputs.' At Home Counties, 'We have taken a very strong position on the values of the organization which are inherently those of an institution which is providing education and training but education contains, if you like, the dominant driving philosophy . . .' Such an official assertion – in the College's mission statement, for instance – of the values of education as a public service 'makes it', as the Principal concluded, 'much more difficult for us in this new climate'.

The new climate and the new funding method in particular demands measurement by results. These performance indicators can be at best indirect approximations of educational quality and as such are liable to manipulation. To take the most fundamental of them for the FEFC funding method, one lecturer admitted to us:

> It may well be that recruitment has gone up but if you look at questions of, in fact, the percentage who genuinely complete a course, I mean . . . in the old days if you like, when we recruited somebody we said we would expect a full-time student to achieve a 75 per cent attendance level, particularly, say for example, if they were on a grant, and this was the general provision. But now we have people and I know a student's mother came to see me yesterday and complained about her daughter and her daughter had a level of attendance of about 12 per cent. Now I can't see that as a full-time student. But that student presumably on the statistics would be seen as being retained and not actually being withdrawn. So, you know again, it depends upon how you interpret the figures and whether you go on the surface or whether you look behind what's going on.

As his colleague added, 'You can do a lot with figures and, of course, since the retention rate influences the funding level then the college is anxious therefore to make the situation appear as bright as possible without verging into the area of the fraudulent.'

We have already seen both managers and lecturers alleging that the funding method led to inappropriate recruitment and a distortion of the college offer towards what was cheap to provide for the largest possible number:

The words that you'll hear quoted are 'high quality, low cost'. In other words, they want it cheap. The only thing you can do cheap are things that don't require consumables, except chalk or pens. So we're looking for areas such as dance and drama which require minimal outlays except floor area [and] many, many students – far more than you can take in most engineering workshops. There's no health and safety problems or very few and you can get the same funding grant from your funding council so it's a very, very easy way to go. So training has gone to low cost and it's not just in this college. Most people are looking towards low-cost courses. (Engineering lecturer)

Don't take on people who won't pass because you don't get your output funding. And that seems to me to be denying the very purpose that FE should be about, given that you're picking up people who've clearly not necessarily succeeded or done well in the school system, who are coming back to look again at education. You should be encouraging and accepting that outcomes can be manifested in a variety of ways, not just by an exam or a certificate. Funding councils have got no way of measuring that. (Middle manager)

This concern tied in with another allegation by several of the lecturer interviewees, and not just those who were sceptical about the rhetoric of change, that:

there seem to be so many initiatives and so many ideas to assist students that it all seems to be widespread rather than in depth. For example, everybody talks about we've got a tutorial system. I'm in charge of a GCSE pathway which in the beginning had about 28 students. Now, I'm their personal tutor and for this I'm given one hour a week. Now, I mean, that's not tutorial support. (GCSE tutor)

As he elaborated:

There are so many buzz words and so many jargon things about action plans and strategies and learning and learning centres etc. but often I think it's just a facade for public consumption and when you look behind at what happens then, in fact, it's just, as I say, it's activity; it looks impressive but there is not much depth in it ... It's, as I say, fashionable to have these things. It looks as if much is going on and it's dynamic and it's vigorous etc., but I would be interested to see whether, in fact, the general experience of students today, in terms of what they get from their courses, not just from the point of view of getting a qualification, but from the point of view of satisfaction and – old-fashioned word – enlightenment, is any superior to what it was five years ago, certainly ten years ago.

This concept of a 'facade' might explain why the appearance of improvement could be so striking to the two students at the end of Chapter 5 who were in a position to make a comparison between the college before and after incorporation. Meanwhile, the teachers claimed that it was only because of their dedication and increased efforts that the appearance of an improved service was presented and that standards had been maintained. So, although 'there's always signs up everywhere' offering students support, for instance, we have also seen from our interviews with students that they did not necessarily take advantage of what was on offer to them. Their teachers too questioned whether students were always confident and motivated enough to use Resource-Based Learning as it was intended. We have also seen lecturers complaining about what they took to be merely 'cosmetic refurbishments'. As another lecturer summed it up, 'The name of the book has changed on the outside label. The content inside is still the same.' Whether this was true or not, it was certainly the case that reliance upon indirect indicators of performance as a way, not only of managing the colleges, but also of responding to the external demands of the Funding Council, made it difficult to determine which were real indicators of improvements in quality and which were virtual ones.

That some of the improvements were real was accepted even by the most intransigent of lecturer interviewees. We have also suggested that positive support tended to be stronger among the newer lecturers and those in subject areas which were growing. Similarly, staff attitudes to an idealized past varied systematically, longer-serving teachers in declining subject areas seeing mainly a falling away from 'the good old days'. By contrast, managers – whilst recognizing that FE, like HE, had been 'a mishmash of brilliance . . . and diabolic practice' – tended to highlight the latter rather than the former. Many of the horror stories which they retailed were associated with baronial rule over the old departments in place of which there was now an attempt at a 'whole college' approach to managing the institution. This was characterized positively as enabling teachers to be much more professionally responsive to the needs of students. Yet again, even where it was agreed by all that there had been real improvements, these changes were perceived as double-edged by the mass of teaching staff. For instance, even when they shared the sense of a new professionalism, embodied in notions of self-direction and responsiveness, this autonomy was circumscribed by the much more systematic monitoring and accountability of lecturers. The two particular areas of load were in relation to the data demanded for the new funding regime and for assessments resulting from the many curricular changes.

So the professionalism of teachers, of which so much was made from both sides of the divide in staff opinions, was in one version a reconstruction of an idealized professional autonomy in a past free of outside interference. This ideal of professionalism was invoked against any further encroachments by management and the outside demands which management were seen to mediate. Management on their side acknowledged this professional ideal in recognizing that it was the dedication to teaching students as a public service that actually kept the corporate college alive in an increasingly competitive market. At the same time, management sought to graft onto the old ideal a new professionalism based upon what they saw as real autonomy, free of the old departmentalism and flexibly networking across boundaries to create a whole-college response to continuing change. This in turn was perceived by main-grade teachers as further encroachment upon their freedom. As one said, 'Tied in with the notion that the institution comes first is the idea that we're cogs in the machine. Us teachers have to accept these changes because, you know, we must love the corporation. There is no choice.' This added to the perception of distance from management even though a hierarchy of many small gradations had been replaced by a 'flattened' one of just a few big steps separating the core SMT from the rest of the staff within the corporate college.

Management led by indicators of output and performance also contributed to what one of the middle managers who was on the whole supportive of his senior management said was 'a kind of dispassionate management . . . which is less about human beings . . . and more about money and numbers . . . a management style which is intensely bureaucratic and cumbersome and non-personal'. As the lecturer he himself line-managed mentioned, 'I mean, "human resource development" is a dead giveaway in terms of their attitude towards the staff. Human beings are not people, they're resources to be utilized by the institution.' Even though this was against the expressed intentions and preferred way of working of the senior management:

> They delegate a lot of stuff down basically to get the work done at a lower level. I mean, the college was set up in a particular way, which is interesting because it's running into problems around it now, but it was set up to be 'democratic' – I use that word in inverted commas really – in that it was trying to get a consensus view of how things were done . . . to try and bring staff with them rather than impose things. In order to do that they've devoted quite a lot of time to creating bodies where people feed things into the system. Quality is a wonderful example. We had a half-day workshop with everybody sitting down trying to work out what their quality standards were. Right, so, you know, a lot of people spent a lot of time – it took a whole college doing this for half a day. They – in each of the programme areas – get together and that gets kind of aggregated into something else and we end up with a set of quality standards that don't bear much relation to the process which we started. Personally at this stage I would rather someone said, 'These are your quality standards. This is what you've got to do' and I would have ended up with more time to do some other things. So I think that's an example of the trying to kind of democratise or trying to have a more of a bottom-up kind of process, which I think these days is rather a luxury really, and I'm not sure how desirable it is when in the end what we're required to do is not within our control. It's actually governed from outside and it's governed by the senior management.

The use of quality indicators as performance targets for indirect management by a contracting core, no longer in direct contact with or control over the actual work being carried out in their institutions, could lead to what can be described as the 'ALL PIGS FLYING' scenario at all levels from Treasury and Funding Council downward through SMT to the shopfloor lecturers. These were the words of a caption to a cartoon one of the authors observed prominently displayed on a noticeboard in one of the colleges. Or, as an interviewee in the other college had it, 'All quality audits present and correct, sir!' Frank Reeves in his book *The Modernity of FE* mentioned in the references to the Introduction, sees such reliance on virtual realities leading logically to the 'virtual college', for, just as industrial managers continue to pursue the impossible goal of a 'workerless factory', Reeves writes:

One fantasy currently exciting management in further education is the possibility of the Marie Celeste college, a silent empty institution of the not-too-distant-future, where every student is enrolled on open and distance learning programmes while payment (enhanced by weighting on load band 3 – FEFC *Guidance on Funding Methodology 1994–95*) is transmitted electronically to the college account.

Colleges ramifying over several 'sites' where students undertake learning in employment, community centres, or at home, are decentring themselves with the danger that, as colleges come to be everywhere, they end up being nowhere, franchising themselves out of existence, for instance.

The commitment of our two colleges to Resource-Based Learning was obviously not intended to produce such a fantastic result and we have also seen the managers of both colleges deplore the franchising of 'virtual courses' by competitor colleges. Nevertheless, the pressure of a remorseless funding regime, every year demanding more for less, may push colleges in this direction if they have nowhere else to turn and want to avoid bankruptcies, mergers and closures. The result will then be, as one of the SMT we interviewed predicted, 'a shift towards a more resource-heavy curriculum in terms of capital resources rather than human resources over time'. Students isolated from other learners might then lose the opportunity for learning from interaction with others that is essential to all learning. For few colleges could support them as elaborately as the Open University which was the ideal model of this type of distance learning; nor were all students – particularly the many new students now entering FE – necessarily as highly motivated or as able to learn for themselves as Open University students.

In addition, as more colleges get into financial difficulties, there will inevitably be more and more mergers and takeovers. These can encourage the drift toward another sense of virtuality in which what we have argued is already a semi-privatized state sector of colleges turns toward full, state-subsidized, privatization, if not of whole institutions then at least of services within them. Already, many colleges employ their growing periphery of part-time and contract teachers through private employment agencies. The Private Finance Initiative, which is proposed by government as the main remaining route to new capital investment, could lead, through financing of buildings and services from private companies, to a situation where a college is a private entity in all but name. Its component services, from catering and cleaning, through to office staff, library, computing and recruitment, etc., could all be contracted out to private providers, some of them doubtless constituted through 'management buy-outs' of the existing staff and resources. The core college managers would then be left running the contracts in the manner of the 'enabling' local authorities advocated by both Conservative and Labour parties. What would then remain of the original public service ideal of the colleges, or of any notion of an entitlement for fee-paying students to enter their local college?

Publishers and software manufacturers may also step in to bid for the provision of teaching materials, assessment and staff and curriculum development. Already, there is a national consortium of more than 150 colleges developing and producing course materials for distribution as hard copy or on CD-ROM. This is at present set up on a charitable basis as a company limited by guarantee but, like the Further Education

Development Agency, which provides management and research support to colleges, it could soon be expected to float free into the marketplace and compete with other providers on a commercial basis. This illustrates a symptomatic problem for the sector (and increasingly for HE and schools as well) for, while such centrally produced learning materials may be of higher quality – especially if they are computer packages, the efficiency savings they enable management to make may be at the expense of lecturers and other staff, leaving students unsupported. Private training agencies or employers themselves have also been encouraged to run their own customized courses on college premises.

We therefore have now to examine the other possibilities open to colleges which our interviewees, among others, have suggested to us. It is also time to face the future of further education by asking honestly whether it has got one.

The future of further education

It can no longer be assumed, as college Principal Vince Hall did in his 1990 survey of *Maintained Further Education in the United Kingdom*, that FE has a natural place in the order of things. So that 'further education is rather like a country, in the middle of a large land mass, which is not bounded by a coastline, a mountain range or a major river'. As such, it has been 'at times partitioned by its large neighbours', but nevertheless, 'has bounced back with a spirit of independence and a will to survive.' It is true that the Poland of FE has always been threatened, not only by the German empire of schools and the Russian bear of higher education, but also by the Austria-Hungary of training. In the 1980s under state sponsorship, the latter example made incursions into the colleges that attempted to wrest 'non-advanced further education' from them. Even though this invasion was eventually repulsed, it left its legacy in the new competence-based assessment as formulated by the NCVQ; and still the scope and reach of the state-subsidized but technically private Training and Enterprise Councils is contested with colleges.

What is new however when we look back over the origin and perpetually perilous history of FE, as briefly outlined in Chapter 1, is that the partial de-industrialization of the UK economy has excluded broad sections of traditionally working-class young people from the labour market and has thus undermined the traditional rationale for FE, namely provision of a non-academic route into skilled jobs. Traditional technical further education thus appears more than ever a relic of the country's ancient industrial past. At the same time, successive governments weakened the power of trade unions, replacing the social partnership of the Industrial Training Boards with employer-dominated Industry Lead Bodies and TECs. Above all, control over funding was taken from LEAs and given to the FEFC. As a result, the local administration of colleges has been replaced by a nationally funded 'market' or 'quasi-market' system of competition for students. The colleges are thus no longer protected from national government learning policies, insofar as these are implemented, for instance, via funding to meet National Targets, or as reflected in Dearing's reviews. The colleges are subject too to government priorities for social security and dealing with the unemployed, as well as being drawn into the incessant battle over pseudo-educational issues conducted in the national media.

This battle is also more virtual than real in the perception of many teachers in schools, and in further and higher education. They can see that education and training has been elevated to a position at the top of the political agenda that is out of all proportion to its real importance in relation to other areas of social policy. This is largely because government can no longer even pretend to do anything about other areas of policy, particularly the economy, over which it has deregulated away effective control. Repetitive argument (at the time of writing centring on proposals to return to the corporal punishment of pupils!), concentrated as ever upon schools, can therefore be asserted to have less to do with any supposed relation to the economy than with attempts to maintain social control. Control over the young and thus over an increasingly uncertain future for society under the nation state, itself changing its form and adjusting to a new global environment, is once again reflected in new millennial moralism (see Chapter 1, p. 3). This moral crusade to draw the youth of a disintegrating social order into a unified national experience is clearly felt by those politicians and parents who are amplified by the media into an orchestrated public opinion, to take place most effectively in schools.

In this respect, though, the UK is out of step with most of the other developed economies of our 'industrial competitors', most of which have school-leaving ages of 18-plus with many more going on to higher education thereafter. Technical education in many European countries often begins in school and can be related there to general, academic learning which is far broader than the narrow English A-level subject specialization in either the arts or the sciences. FE has no overseas counterpart save in the Anglo-Saxon Antipodes and in the related but different form of the community colleges in the USA. Nor does FE fit easily with the varied education and training structures of mainland Europe. FE colleges are still 'unique institutions', as the Ministry of Education once described them, endorsing a confident 'Future Development of Higher Technological Education' after the Second World War. 'Certainly not to be found either in the United States of America or most countries on the Continent of Europe.' Like some other peculiarities of the English, this uniqueness could be seen as less of a strength and more of a weakness.

It could also be argued that FE has little place in the latest 'learning policy', as we referred to it in Chapter 1. This policy is supposedly intended to respond more effectively to a deregulated global economy. However, many of the recent reforms have little to do with any supposed correspondence of education of any type to the economy. Rather, they are an attempt to restore through education a world that has been lost, where clear social divisions separated mental from manual labour and, within the last category, the skilled from the unskilled working class. These divisions have of course been eroded not only by the loss of the heavy industrial base which sustained them and the latest applications of information and communication technologies but also by the growth of comprehensive schooling since 1964 and before. The Conservative reforms of education, particularly the 1988 Education Act, were widely seen as an attempt to restore that blue-remembered past and to bring back grammar schools under the guise of encouraging 'diversity' and 'excellence', eventually openly endorsing 'a grammar school in every town' before the 1997 general election. Exhortations to 'parity of esteem' between diverse pathways therefore rang as hollow as when the phrase was first applied to the three types of secondary state school – grammar, technical and modern – to which pupils were allocated at 11-plus by IQ testing after the Second World War.

Like the other Conservative reforms of the welfare state, the declared aim of what government came to call 'an efficiently operating learning market' was to achieve higher standards by motivating parents and pupils/students at all levels of learning. This would, it was intended, create a system of 'ladders and bridges' between pathways whereby individuals could gain academic and vocational qualifications and continue to progress throughout their lives to increase personal opportunity and contribute to wealth generation. This would in turn create what the government called a 'learning society' by the year 2000, that is a society which would (in the formulation it was given) systematically increase the knowledge and skills of all its members to exploit technological innovation and so gain a competitive edge for their services in fast-changing global markets. Such a development is advocated because the industrial competitiveness of the UK is widely accepted as being dependent upon a highly skilled workforce, able to innovate and to produce goods and services of a high marketable value. In a competitive global market, it is argued, developed countries like Britain can no longer compete in the mass production of the heavy industrial goods with which they once led the world; especially as newly industrializing economies, like the islands of the Pacific rim, are followed not only by countries like South Korea and Malaysia but by the giant economies of China, India and Indonesia.

Now in order to sell it is necessary for the already developed economies to produce for specialized and niche markets in high technology goods and services. These require a workforce that is computer literate rather than merely functionally literate and numerate, as was needed for the first industrial revolution. At the same time, the rapid pace of technical change demands workers who are able to adapt flexibly to new technology throughout their working lives. The citizens of a learning society would thus exercise an individual entitlement to lifelong learning, education and training no longer being 'front-loaded' upon the young.

In such a 'learning society', individuals would be continually investing in their own human capital through education and training programmes during varied and flexible careers. Indeed, the Confederation of British Industry's 1994 policy document 'Thinking Ahead' celebrates this type of occupational fluidity alongside the suggestion that graduates and other qualified individuals should no longer expect to have secure employment for life. Rather, they will build up portfolios of occupational experiences, moving from one 'challenging' project to the next. So, for the CBI, 'learning to learn' thus becomes the only constant in a constantly changing world. In such a vision, FE would seem after all to find a necessary place, characterized as it is by its voluntary and uniquely flexible and responsive form to provide for a variety of individuals in new and changing situations. This is the basis for an optimistic and modernizing scenario for the future of FE related closely to the economy and opposed to the social control agenda for education of reversing into the future by attempting to restore the past that was lately advocated by the Conservative government.

'The role of government in this world of change', as defined by the leader of the 'new' Labour Party, writing in *The New Statesman* (29 September 1995) 'is to represent a national interest, to create a competitive base of physical infrastructure and human skills . . . to educate and retrain for the next technologies, to prepare our country for new global competition, and to make our country a competitive base from which to produce the goods and services people want to buy.' Such is the unanimity of agreement on this response to global change that the 1995 European Union White Paper on education and training, 'Towards the Learning Society' can declare 'The end of debate on educational principles.'

Whether coming from the once dominant modernizing faction of Conservative government supported by the CBI, or from New Labour and the trade union leaders, this solution to Britain's social and economic progress rests upon the related assumption of the need for a general 'upskilling' in the labour force. However, whether the UK workforce as a whole is becoming more or less skilled and knowledgeable is debatable. Indeed, Conservative governments were often criticized for following a contrary policy. In seeking to attract foreign capital looking to invest in assembling and servicing in Britain as a bridgehead to the European heartland, successive Tory governments emphasized the virtues of a low-wage, deregulated workforce. As a result, Britain now has the lowest labour costs per unit of output of any industrialized country, the US being second. Similarly, work reorganization with consequent labour shedding plus 'culture change' and work intensification for those remaining in employment, rather than job satisfaction for all employees, are often the goals of employer involvement in education and training programmes. These programmes usually accompany the introduction of new information and communication technologies and new methods of working in their organizations.

Far fewer people are now required to operate machinery that is as phenomenally productive as it is phenomenally expensive. This has contributed to permanent, structural unemployment, so that millions of people are relegated to insecure, part-time, intermittent and semi-skilled labour, if they are lucky. Education and training, it has often been said, have been expanded to take up the slack. At one level, are those on programmes requiring participation in training or work experience as a condition of receipt of welfare or unemployment benefits. At another are those whose pre-existing cultural capital is legitimated by elite higher education. Between these two extremes lie the mass of students and trainees, adults as well as younger people, whose participation in education and training is often prompted by unemployment or the fear of it. This has implications for the motivation that is widely recognized as crucial to learning.

Knowledge and skill are polarizing in line with new divisions of labour. For, in the new labour market only a core of secure workers actually use higher level knowledge and skills in employment. A growing periphery of semi-skilled, insecure, part-time employees have no need for further learning to carry out the deskilled, routine tasks much labour continues to demand, especially in the expanded service sector of the economy. Yet many more people now have to possess education certificates both to find and keep paid work – as at least one of our student interviewees could see very clearly (p. 95).

The 'vision' of the former Manpower Services Commission, allied as it was to the modernizing faction of Conservative governments, therefore appears to have been contradicted both by the actual development of a deregulated labour market on the ground and by education policies which seek to 'reverse into the future' by reintroducing tripartite distinctions associated with former divisions of labour and class. Yet a modernizing agenda to which FE might respond in the flexible manner for which it is uniquely fitted is still represented by the CBI and the 'learning society' ideal. The 'new' Labour Party also sometimes talks in modernizing terms. Like the Conservatives though, some statements by New Labour tend to hark back to an idealized tripartite past at the same time as proposing a vision of classless and meritocratic modernization that ignores the reality of permanent structural unemployment. Or, rather, as with the openly espoused monetarist policies of Conservative governments, unemployment is surreptitiously used to motivate the workforce through workfare measures that have replaced the social insurance principle of the old welfare state premised upon demand management to maintain full employment. The 'learning society' notion of both Tory and Labour modernizers is thus linked to the 'active society' approach to welfare reform in tandem with the 'active labour market policies' advocated by the OECD and the World Bank.

So none of the Parliamentary parties propose a real alternative for education and training to either of these two confused approaches of retreat and modernization. To do so would raise the demand for full but not full-time employment and the necessity to integrate learning not only with earning but also with leisure. Such an alternative policy would begin the transformation of values that are necessary for humanity's survival in the new millennium and which begin by challenging what has been called 'The Dogma of Work'. We have suggested that, despite the vocational pressures upon them, many in the new mass of students working their way through further, higher and continuing education and training are beginning to shape such a challenge in the ways in which they struggle to make lives for themselves in the circumstances in which they find themselves.

At present, paid employment is presented to them as the only way in which to achieve personal fulfilment, yet, against these narrowly vocational and entrepreneurial obsessions, many people would agree with Professor Mike Cooley of Bremen University that

> The year 2000 could and should provide a powerful stimulus to examine where, as an industrial society, we are going. To do so at a macro level, we will require the perspective of a historian, the imagination of a poet, the analytic ability of a scientist, and the wisdom of a Chief Seattle . . . [For] It seems self-evident that developing the skill and knowledge necessary in the twenty-first century will require nothing short of a 'cultural and industrial renaissance' . . . [and that] Our current educational systems are fundamentally inappropriate and woefully inadequate to address this historical task.

Far from beginning to address such essential concerns, the environment in which education in general, and FE in particular, operates precludes any consideration of long-term issues. For what we have called the Contracting State, exemplified by the funding mechanism for further education, is characterized above all by inherent short-termism concentrated upon meeting quantitative performance targets. As these reduce qualitative judgements of value to numerical formulation they become emptied of all real meaning, let alone any relation to the economy.

In this respect also, there is no essential difference between the approaches to the economy and to learning of both main parties. Conservative governments from 1979 introduced the new form of state. Instead of what could be called the old, Corporate State corresponding to the former mixed economy with its social partners brought together by social democratic government, a new Contracting State has been introduced. This apt formulation captures the dual sense in which the state is contracting, both as to its mode of operation by franchise or contract and by its increasingly centralized and concentrated power. Ironically, this centralization of power occurs as supra-national political and economic entities, like the European Union and the North American Free Trade Association, usurp many of the traditional functions of the old nation state. Still, the nation state remains crucial to the shape that globalization takes locally. It also remains the main forum for political accountability and therefore the focus of pressures for change.

The new Contracting State is, however, increasingly untrammelled by the obligations of either social partnership or of even representative democracy as it substitutes for them the global market to which it has opened itself as the sole arbiter of public accountability. The new form of indirect state regulation allows central direction to be concentrated whilst reducing the apparent responsibility of government and shielding policy from representative channels of accountability. Instead of democracy, contract is increasingly substituted for representation and consumer charters are substituted for membership. This shifts the responsibility for policy effectiveness from government's shoulders and blurs the location of responsibility for failure.

The new Contracting State system thus not only disorganizes dissent but has been set up as if deliberately to self-destruct as funding for it is cut. We have seen in further education how continuing convergence on a reduced unit of resource threatens disaster for the whole sector. Yet the FEFC argues that it is not part of its remit to plan. Colleges' strategic plans, approved by the local TECs, are merely 'assessed' by the FEFC, as it says in its latest 'Corporate Plan 1996–97 – 1998–99: 'to satisfy itself that it is meeting its statutory duty to ensure that sufficient and adequate facilities for further education are made available to meet the needs of the labour market and employers at national, regional and local levels'.

However, 'sufficient and adequate' remains undefined. Meanwhile, two thirds of the colleges owed debts totalling £82 million, according to the FEFC in August 1996, and around 70 colleges were reported to be technically insolvent. In February 1997, the National Audit Office reported 83 colleges unable to cover their financial liabilities for 1995–96, 280 colleges in deficit during 1995–96 (as compared with 214 in 1993–94) and four out of ten colleges unable to guarantee to the FEFC that they could control their own finances. These are the same colleges previously identified as weak by accountants Coopers and Lybrand. Management consultants, Peat Marwick, also predicted that one in five colleges would close or merge – similar to the lecturers' union, NATFHE's estimates. We have discussed the reasons why some of these worst case scenarios have not already come to pass but we would not therefore be optimistic that they will not occur in the future (see p. 113).

Similar funding systems are producing similar results elsewhere in the Contracting State: in the health service, for instance, on 17 May 1996 *The Guardian* reported 'Hospitals head for meltdown' under accounting rules 'that mean hospitals must charge less and less each year for their services'. The Conservative government averted hospital closures only by drip-feeding the NHS with extra cash in the run-up to the 1997 general election. It is likely therefore that there will be further reductions in public services, on the one hand, together with privatizations, on the other, of the parts of services that can be run profitably and which only a minority of customers will then be able to afford. The dismantling of the welfare state will thus continue apace. In the case of hospitals there may be powerful local campaigns that contest closures but we cannot hope the same for FE colleges or even universities.

In the competition between schools and colleges, the academic route was confirmed in Dearing's first two reviews as the high road to higher education via school sixth forms. FE cannot console itself that it at present teaches the majority of A-level candidates, for this could change if schools build up their sixth forms. In addition, many school sixth formers are also taking the low road to HE through the more vocationally related former polytechnics, while NVQs are intended for learning in employment. NVQs could be increasingly provided independently of FE colleges on employer premises. With the exception of some Modern Apprenticeships, work-based training is much cheaper to run than either college provision or the even higher cost of retaining students in schools (even though even fewer trainees complete to qualification than do students in college or at school). Indeed, the government's 1994 'Competitiveness' Mark 1 White Paper emphasized the role of the employer-based TECs and LECs rather than the colleges in the delivery of work-based training.

By introducing GNVQs into schools at age 14 in his first review, Dearing signalled a place in FE for those who fail the academic National Curriculum. This was confirmed by the suggestion in his second review of a 'work-based' route for 'non-academic' 14-year-olds. This would revive previous 'link courses' that many colleges ran in association with schools, providing practical activities and other opportunities for learning not only for special school students but also for pupils seeking an alternative to standard school exam courses. However, such collaboration between schools and colleges is very rare nowadays due to competition for students and the difficulties under present arrangements of transferring payment from schools under local financial management to the corporate colleges. This proposal by Dearing was plainly ill-thought-out and is unworkable. Yet, by associating FE with school failure, it enhances the status and esteem of school sixth forms vis-à-vis the colleges.

Keeping young people in school meets the public concern for control over youth. This is plainly felt to be more effectively exercised by teachers in small school sixth forms rather than in large and anonymous colleges, without school uniforms and in which students enjoy the freedom and self-responsibility we found so many of them remarking upon so positively. Under the 1996 Education Act, now passing through Parliament, grant maintained schools are to be encouraged to open sixth forms without having to seek permission from the Secretary of State for Education – also signalling the type of state schools in which the Conservatives particularly favour sixth forms.

At the same time as FE is encroached upon by schools in this manner, HE threatens to colonize it from the other direction. Some former polytechnics, together with other higher education institutions confined mainly to teaching in the hierarchy of competing universities, have proposed amalgamations with FE colleges. Thus, the University of Derby, for example, suggested a federation with eight local FE colleges (later reduced to two or three). The University of Central England (UCE) discussed amalgamation with East Birmingham College, and Worcester College of Higher Education absorbed Kidderminster College, while East Birmingham and Clarendon Colleges already run two-year associate degrees with UCE and Nottingham Trent University. Staffordshire University federated with Newcastle-under-Lyme College and shares a site with Lichfield and Tamworth Colleges.

Many of these proposals for further/higher education mergers were vetoed by the FEFC and we have suggested this was an instance of the Council's protective stance towards what Sir William Stubbs saw as its colleges. It was also an indication that, with Dearing's 16–19 report, the tide in favour of HE turned instead to a bias in favour of schools to the neglect of FE. The previous discussion of the benefits of a unitary Further and Higher Education Funding Council was also shelved (perhaps temporarily). Nevertheless, other higher education institutions have incorporated various monotechnic colleges as parts of themselves, as Brunel University the West London Institute, or De Montfort the Lincolnshire Colleges of Art and Agriculture. Similarly, Coventry University and the city's College of Performing Arts have joined forces, as have Portsmouth University and Portsmouth College of Art. All the schools of nursing and colleges of health have also found their way into associations if not amalgamations with universities.

Moreover, HE enjoys a long-term, built-in advantage over FE. As Sir Toby Weaver once wisely remarked, asking 'Higher than What, Further than Where?' in a lecture at Rotherham College of Technology in 1974: 'in a meritocratic society, which all too readily interprets "higher" as a measure of social status rather than intellectual achievement . . . to travel further is accounted of less merit than to climb higher'. It should be pointed out, however, that, for all the chatter from academics about a 'mass' higher education system, which for many of them remains a contradiction in terms, HE actually still caters for only 30 per cent of 18-plus-year-olds (though more in Scotland). FE reached this extent of 'mass' partipation long ago and now, together with schools, accounts for approximately two thirds of 16–18-year-olds, a medium if not, as we said, a mass participation post-compulsory education.

So, although the FE colleges' growth has been unprecedented, their present position is more than usually ambiguous and their future even more uncertain than it has ever been. A pattern of mergers prompted by reductions in local government expenditure that began in the 1980s with three colleges into one on the Wirral and eight into one in Liverpool, leaves the continued existence of many small colleges uncertain – the ten small colleges in Leeds, for instance. However, size is not everything; some large colleges are in financial difficulties and some small ones are thriving. For instance, a few sixth-form colleges have merged with tertiary or generalist FE colleges while others, especially in the old sixth-form centres and former grammar schools, are booming. Nevertheless, economies of scale are possible for large institutions under the new funding arrangements and so, in the absence of more coherent arrangements, mergers have become a form of planning by default as well as the ultimate outcome of competition between colleges. In Spring 1997, the *Times Educational Supplement* reported 'the merger of Gateshead and Newcastle Colleges is certain to be seen as the start of a new phase of mergers in FE' (7 March).

Mergers between formerly scattered specialist technical colleges are augmented by the tendency noted above for higher education institutions, which are also – particularly the former polytechnics – in competition for students both with each other and with FE colleges, to secure their supply of local students by associating with neighbouring FE colleges. A reported and predictable attraction to Dearing's review of HE of following an Americanized model of FE colleges as junior colleges to associated universities to which students move to complete their degrees, is that it is much cheaper to deliver some HE in FE.

So where does this leave FE in Britain today? It appears to be facing disadvantageous competition with schools and HE, while the latest FEFC Corporate Plan advocates a reduction in funding of 'at least 5 per cent each year'. The inevitable detrimental results of these measures can only be averted by a deliberate choice of government. For while there are important differences remaining between funding for schools, further and higher education, free market competition in FE has gone further than in any other sector of education and its consequences are clearer there than anywhere else. This is another reason that makes it important for those outside FE to appreciate what is going on in the neglected sector.

The lessons learnt from FE can be taken two ways. Either they are an awful warning to avoid the predictable outcome of contract funding on a reducing unit of resource leading to closures and mergers. Or the new government may be tempted to apply a similar funding method regardless to all schools, further and higher education and training, under a unified and possibly voucherized system disguised as a form of 'learning credit' perhaps linked to a 'Learning Bank'. This would have the apparent virtues of 'fairness' and toughness with which the FEFC funding regime was announced. This is the real choice facing the new government – whether to sustain and extend the Contracting State in education as elsewhere, or to turn towards a real alternative to it.

Our interviewees, both managers and teachers, in Inner City and Home Counties Colleges were clear which option they preferred. The two Principals – both of whom had reservations about incorporation when it was first proposed – 'would', as one said, 'want to go back to a world of regional planning' with 'regional specialisms' and 'local generalisms', 'a planned staged entitlement'. As the other stated:

> The objective is actually to agree what the proper profile of colleges should be across the country. That would be a legitimate aim, it seems to me, of leadership of the sector that says resources are disappearing, can't afford to waste resources, can't afford unnecessary and stupid competition – I'm spending £20,000 on marketing, so is the guy next door so that we can cancel each other out. That's £40,000 down the tubes. Whereas, if we were a single college with a single catchment area we would still have to spend something but we would save a significant amount. That sort of thing is crazy.

Indeed, such unnecessary duplication and waste encouraged by competition between colleges was unanimously deplored by all staff interviewees. As was, as we have seen in the interviews with the teachers, the tendency of the present funding method to encourage what was cheaply deliverable irrespective of community, student or employer need.

Regional planning and 'relatively small colleges joining together' would, other members of the SMT at both colleges felt, regain 'the sense of FE as a sector' that had been lost:

> I think we won't be a sector in the future and I personally feel that's a loss because I think our power and our strength is in us being a sector. I think you can be a sector and I think you can celebrate your diversity so I don't think a sector means we're one thing. I think a sector can mean that we are the whole spread of things that's within the sector from the old, what were the old, tech colleges, to the tertiaries, to the FEs; so I think we can be different within it but still be a sector. And I feel that there isn't anything at all that is actually looking at us as a sector and what the needs of us as a sector would be and I think that's right from the level of staff progression across the country within the sector to what is the sector about and what does it need in the future.

'Some kind of planning structure' for the FE sector could amount to a form of manpower planning, suggested one manager, 'in which we will need to look at how many people we want to be trained in social care, carpentry, bricklaying and accountancy and then ask the sector to provide those so that perhaps then resources would follow those sorts of targets'. Such planning might be 'top down to some extent' but it would also need 'some regional basis to it', '. . . to ensure that colleges within a common economic area are complementary to each other'. This might lead, thought another manager, to 'regional technical colleges, strategically placed around the country . . . there's nothing new about it. It's back to the early 1950s.'

However, management all agreed on opposing any return to regions as small as the LEAs. They opposed the 'interference', bureaucracy and party politics that predictably prioritized schools under the old local council control. They considered that this would jeopardize the real improvements in service to students, their communities and employers made since incorporation. By contrast, many of the teaching staff whom we interviewed advocated a return to the local authorities, not least because they represented a form of democratic control as opposed to 'unaccountable quangos' of 'men in suits', or 'the bankers' as one main-grade lecturer referred to his college's board of governors. For the same reasons, along with an end to incorporation, they also advocated a return to and extension of more democratic involvement by staff and students with rights to representation on the governing bodies of the colleges in which they worked and studied. From this perspective:

> Incorporation is a complete misnomer. They should have called it excorporation. You know, it appears to be the FE equivalent of opting-out and they have to call it incorporation because opting-out involved an element of choice and incorporation didn't. But basically they're the same thing – secondary schools opt out and FE colleges which have become incorporated are actually moving into central government control.

What neither group considered was an alternative that would combine democratic control with the regional administration favoured by managers. This was doubtless because such a combination would entail other constitutional changes to decentralize and democratize the state and introduce changes to local/regional government going far beyond the immediate predicament of further education. Yet such proposals have been advanced by the EU as part of the vision of 'a Europe of the regions'. The Labour Party is also committed to Regional Development Agencies. They are also part of the agenda of the local and regional coalitions represented by the 'Learning Cities' movement that attempts to bring together and sustain public education and training against the fragmenting effects of competition within the Contracting State, as well as being concerned with issues of public order. A number of private companies and even transnational corporations have also been involved in these efforts.

The power of new information and communication technologies to reach large numbers of learners in very different circumstances is common to many of these 'Campaigns for Learning'. This, we have seen, was also a part of the new agenda for colleges and was suggested by some interviewees as a way out from the current crisis of the sector, taking administrative pressure off teachers and leaving them free to teach, or rather to facilitate learning which in its routine forms would be computer-aided. Yet they also agreed that the use of computer-aided learning packages and similar educational technologies should be an additional resource for students, not a substitute for regular scheduled teaching sessions with lecturers.

These suggestions were made by interviewees as part of a more hopeful future for further education than the various worst-case scenarios we have sketched out above. Many interviewees at all levels looked to a period of 'bedding down' for the changes that had already occurred. Managers in particular we have seen anticipating an ongoing 'culture change' amongst their staffs as acceptance of the new realities permeated 'down a layer' and as new staff replaced old-timers. They all thus hoped for relief from the 'endless pressure' that many managers as well as main-grade interviewees spoke of as so 'remorseless'. Yet they also expected that the relentless series of transformations focused upon the sector would inevitably continue. Nevertheless, some remained optimistic and indicated support for an optimal future for mass further education. For there are signs of widespread agreement, not only as reflected by our interviewees but across the FE sector as a whole, on an alternative and viable way forward that can be said to constitute a new but, as yet, largely unarticulated consensus. It is to this optimistic scenario that we now turn.

The value of further education

The nascent new consensus asserts the value of further education for the future development of learning as a whole. It centres on a shared vision of the potential development of the colleges in concert with schools, higher education and training. Together, they can provide structures through which communities facing traumatic economic and social change can learn to survive.

In this sense, the implicit possibilities of the two alternatives represented by the two different types of tertiary and generalist college which have been the subject of this book are reduced to one best way forward. This is towards a comprehensive post-compulsory sector of state schools and colleges in which there is progression and transfer between curriculum pathways which are not tied to particular types of institution. In other words and in principle, students – adults as well as school-leavers – should be able to follow any course, whether academic, generally vocational or specifically work-related, in, or in association with any FE college or school sixth form. They should also be able to combine their subjects of study across institutions, just as students who were based in school sixth forms used to have the opportunity to attend college for part of their time. In a similar way, students – whether at school or college – often also undertake learning *from* work – if not always learning *to* work – and trainees from work have traditionally been 'released' to colleges. FE colleges have particular traditional strengths that can be built upon with a polytechnic emphasis upon the applied and the vocational. They also run other courses which often require investment in expensive resources and equipment that can be concentrated in their sites. With its well-established comprehensive offer at all levels, FE should not be confined to vocational study. As it is, much academic work – both A-level and HE – already occurs in colleges.

This is to recognize that the opportunity to move nationally towards post-16 tertiary colleges, which we described as being lost at the end of the 1970s, is irrecoverable. The development of sixth forms in schools as well as sixth-form colleges has gone too far to be universally reversed into the straitjacket of transfer to tertiary institutions at 16-plus. (Indeed, accepting this keeps open the possibility of establishing for as many people as possible the normality and desirability of full-time education with US-style graduation from a 'high school' base with a leaving qualification at 18 and recurring returns to learning full- and part-time thereafter.) Instead of old-style tertiary colleges, a variety of post-16 schools and colleges can be recognized as providing the basis for a new form of tertiary education linked across institutions. This would check any tendency towards a new tripartism at tertiary level in which students followed different pathways in separate institutions. To prevent this development by allowing not only progression within pathways but inter-relation and transfer between them, competition for students between rival providers has to be ended. This will give students real choice, unhampered by the competing blandishments of schools and colleges. To make this a reality, funding will have to be equitable between schools and colleges with some kind of unified management ensuring co-operation within a given locality.

To create such a state-supported learning infrastructure will require not only relating the schools within a region or sub-region to their colleges but the colleges to local higher education. Universities and other higher education institutions are also undergoing transformations similar to those which have been described for further education, especially since the removal of the binary barrier against the former polytechnics. Under conditions of open competition for students, this is leading towards the reinstatement of a new division between an elite of academic, research universities and the rest. Whilst this development needs to be checked, it is equally predictable that, as is already beginning in FE, mergers if not closures of higher education institutions are likely. This will lead to large mega-universities that can become the hub of the learning infrastructure in their regions to which local colleges will be affiliated, as in turn schools can be inter-related with their local college.

The idea of infrastructural development is emphasized here as a learning infrastructure that will be as essential to creating a real learning society as is transport or an adequate health service to social and economic functioning today. As stated by the last Labour Chancellor, Denis Healey, 'For Britain the first priority must be a massive switch from defence spending and arms manufacture to economic reconstruction. Otherwise we cannot hope to repair the damage done in recent years to our economic infrastructure – our roads and railways, our schools, colleges and universities.' Such a learning infrastructure, which includes the new hardware and software of the latest communications and information technology in all media, should not be seen as merely relating to economic development. It has just as vital a role to play in developing popular leisure, sport, recreation and the arts from which too much officially sanctioned learning at all levels has for too long been divorced. This would be expensive, but only such a redirection of resources can prepare the way for a culture of lifelong learning and recurrent access to further, higher and adult learning; a culture that would create opportunities to provide education and training for the 70 per cent of the current workforce who have not acquired any worthwhile qualifications, as well as for the four million people seeking work (as opposed to being officially registered unemployed). With the 1991 White Paper 'Employment and Training for the Twenty-first Century' focused almost exclusively upon young people, the 3.4 million adults enrolled in further and adult education have once again been forgotten. And again, the Conservative government's free-market dogma negated its vocational training rhetoric, for the economy has been so run down that FE has become the last refuge for much skill training in local labour markets. Yet with investment in the technology, schools, colleges and universities could respond to the gathering pace of technological change which requires a corresponding programme of retraining throughout employees' careers.

Secondary schools, it often seems, have a lot to answer for in not realizing the aspirations of youngsters – as instanced, for example, by several of the Foundation-level interviewees in our two colleges. This has much to do with the way secondary schooling sorts people by examination in limited and largely literary competences for entry to the labour market. It also has to do with the way schools have developed in modern times to separate young people for lengthening periods from the rest of society, which they can then only study in an abstract and theoretical manner. Linking schools not only with colleges and universities but with home and other out-of-school sites of learning will change our idea of the school as being the single discrete institution in which education takes place once and for all. Not only getting youngsters learning out of school but more adults learning and helping to teach in school will ease many of the problems now faced by secondary education particularly. It will also help to develop a more radical conception of a 'Learning Society' in which all areas of social life can become sites of learning and all social institutions have an educational function.

The new learning infrastructure of inter-related schools, colleges and universities can be developed on a regional basis with devolved funding on the European model. This means the end of the attempt to run a national system through centralized funding. The FEFC will have to be replaced by regional funding bodies. This is because the Funding Council does not see its colleges as integral parts of all-through education and training which starts in schools and converges in a communal spirit spurred by the public service ethos of comprehensive provision, but as isolated and competing institutions. This means it cannot in fact ensure that all school-leavers have access to the whole range of learning provided by a network of comprehensive colleges in co-operation with the sixth forms in their areas. Similarly, the market in education in which the FEFC operates is unable to provide the reorganization that is required for it forces institutions to specialize unnecessarily and to provide what is fundable rather than what is needed by students, communities and industry. Meanwhile other colleges go to the wall and the system as a whole polarizes increasingly.

In addition to the replacement of the FEFC, a comprehensive state learning infrastructure will also require radical transformation of the Training and Enterprise Councils/Local Enterprise Companies. This would return all oversight and resources relating to education for the 16 to 19 age group to the public education service, with funding transferred to regional budgets. Not only would this mean that work-related learning could be overseen democratically but it would unify the learning of all 16–18-year-olds within a single system. Employers would be able to buy in to this state-supported learning infrastructure through a levy of the type they used to pay to the Industrial Training Boards. For the state cannot expect employers to take the lead in education and training that they do not see it as their business to provide. Even though most training is undertaken in firms, increasingly non-specific and 'transferable' training in the generic tasks becoming common to all industries and services with the diffusion to them of new information and communications technologies, has to be undertaken as a public service in schools, colleges and universities. The speed with which training and retraining is required for all members of the workforce if they are to keep up with transformations of technology only heightens the perennial problem of coaching and poaching – when one employer poaches employees coached at the expense of another. This can be alleviated through a unified and state-supported learning infrastructure of which the FE colleges with their expertise in the inter-relations of learning to earning would be a vital part.

Integrity of provision of learning is important not because it is administratively convenient but because it permits the unification of the academic with the vocational curriculum in a national framework for credit accumulation and transfer in which transfer between 'pathways' would exist for the first time. The Further Education Unit of the Department of Education had developed the outline and principles of a credit accumulation framework for post-16 learning in 'A Basis for Credit' in 1992. Similar proposals have been elaborated for higher education, for example by Professor Robertson of Liverpool John Moores University in his 1994 'Choosing to Change'. This envisages a modular system explicitly extended from higher to further education, as already exists in Fforum, the Welsh qualifications framework. The Scottish system of five higher sixth-form examinations has also been made continuous with general vocational and vocational qualifications and the 'Higher Still' proposals suggest extending this to all higher education. This provides an already existing model for modularizing A-levels as a first step to broaden sixth-form study and integrate it with general vocational learning to facilitate progression and transfer. Similar proposals for such a broad-based diploma were developed in *A British Baccalaureate, Ending the Division Between Education and Training*, published in the London-based Institute for Public Policy Research in 1990.

'Qualifications', as Caroline Benn and Clyde Chitty point out in their 1996 survey of comprehensive education that includes the FE sector, 'are vital but they are not the sole cure' for reform. For, as they say, while new methods of assessment are required, there is still the matter of institutional reorganization. They suggest that comprehensive reorganization for the 16 to 19 age group is not being discussed 'possibly for fear that it would mean ending the sixth form'. Yet, as they argue: 'With every passing year the case for reorganization of the 16 to 19 stage is making itself, as increasing problems arise within a completely unreformed institutional structure fractured by divisions and differentiated funding, dominated by uneconomic sixth forms, private sector training agencies and a general further education sector wherein all schools and colleges must compete (though their wish is often to co-operate).' 'Instead of getting simpler', this results in the 16–19 system becoming 'more of a jungle than ever'. For, they add: 'institutional arrangements are becoming ever more complex, and the system ever more selective. The competition that is supposed to fuel development isn't real competition, for it is heavily controlled and manipulated by the centralized state' (pp. 383–4)

We can only endorse their recommendations for the 'principles for a new system' which, as they say, are 'relatively simple':

> Integration of the curriculum; a common assessment and accreditation system; and full progression for all within a common framework. In terms of institutional organization there would be no selection for institutions individually but each (by mutual negotiation under the auspices of the local or regional authority) would have as full a range of study and students as possible. No one institution could offer every course and qualification, but together all could offer that other essential of a comprehensive education: all that is normally expected for the age range as a whole. To these must be added the duty of the service to accommodate part-timers on an equal basis with full-timers, and, as time continues, to be open to adults of all ages as well.

All this, they recognize:

> Would not happen overnight. There are too many 'holes' in provision and too much inequality in the system to reorganize instantly. But with electorally accountable bodies given the duty to undertake the work, it could be accomplished in a lot less than the 30 years it took the 11–16 years in state schools to end selection and achieve comprehensive-compatible curricula and assessment. It would involve developing most general FE colleges to 'network' the country, each college allied to local sixth forms of schools or sixth-form colleges. More and more FE colleges would then become tertiary colleges but even without this development the system could be built around sixth forms and FE colleges working co-operatively. What counts would be a common tertiary administration where courses would be available within the network to learners wherever based. (p. 389)

This is the outline of a new form of comprehensive tertiary education to which mass further education can aspire. Benn and Chitty's proposals for moving towards it are practicable step-by-step solutions which the new government could begin to implement. They are not Utopian, yet they are set within a broad vision. Part of the possibilities towards which they point is indicated by their assertion that 'For the first time in almost two centuries there is the possibility of our society reshaping itself democratically because there is the possibility of reshaping work itself' (p. 379). Work is already being transformed by the latest applications of information and communication technologies and it is common to speak of a new industrial revolution with historic implications even more profound than the first industrial revolution.

The institutions that have been examined in this book have developed from their roots in the first industrial revolution. We have seen the FE college's unique adaptability and responsiveness to economic and social change, elaborating new kinds of provision as needed by changing local industries and communities. The FE colleges are thus a unique national resource. They are the nearest that the country has to institutions, for educating the whole community, making vocational and academic learning more accessible than either schools or higher education to returners to learning at all levels. Especially to adults and others 'failed' by schools and universities, the colleges have traditionally afforded a second chance to learn. This is the value of further education, yet it is not widely appreciated, even within the education community, let alone by politicians and media fixated upon schools.

By looking in detail at just two colleges, we have presented a picture of this uniquely valuable sector of education under unprecedented pressure as a result of being subjected to a central government experiment in quasi-marketization. This has pioneered in FE as a whole the new contractual arrangements of the new type of state system. The FEFC funding method, which has been the instrument of this policy, has 'destabilized further education', in the words of Lambeth College Principal, Adrian Perry. It has forced managers to push through new contracts with their staffs to get more work for less out of fewer teachers in order for colleges to survive. As evidenced by our interviews with them in Chapter 4, this has considerably distracted teachers from their real business of teaching.

Also, the establishment of systems to manage finance and information demanded by the new funding method has also diverted money that should have been spent on teaching towards a new bureaucracy. The resulting demands upon staff, and the competition they are in with other providers is, as we have seen, not only stressful for all concerned but also often wasteful and unnecessary. All this has occurred in the context of year-on-year reductions of taught hours for students. As a result, the very future of the further education sector is more than ever uncertain. For, after a brief moment of glory, which we recalled in Chapter 2, when there was money available for growth, even at reduced amounts per student, caps and cuts in both capital and recurrent funding followed almost immediately.

Nevertheless, it has to be recognized that the new funding method has achieved control over the allocation of resources for the first time and ironed out some gross disparities which existed between colleges. There is no going back to the good old/bad old days. The offer of recognition for FE to find its place and importance acknowledged for the first time in a national system of education and training, though it was quickly withdrawn, has drawn attention to the disparities in funding for students in schools, further and higher education. Moreover, not only have student numbers increased dramatically but facilities have been improved, along with the course offer to many students and trainees. However, these real improvements cannot be jeopardized any longer by remorseless convergence of funding on a reduced unit of resource. This has already led to a real crisis for many colleges.

As John Akker, President of the lecturers' union, NATFHE, warns in the April 1997 issue of *The Lecturer*, 'the system of FE set up by the Further and Higher Education Act 1992 is in deep crisis. This could end in its destruction, or at the very least lasting damage to much of the education and training infrastructure.' 'The collapse of further education' he foresees is no over-dramatic or self-interested prediction. There are 450 colleges – though the number is steadily reducing – that face severe challenges in the cut-throat competition unleashed upon them. The workings and consequences of these new legal and financial arrangements were revealed to us in our two colleges by those most immediately involved, their staffs and students.

To respond to the crisis in further education will demand a concerted and united campaign by the colleges. Yet we have shown how it was not until 1996, faced with the results of their sudden aggregation as individual and independent corporations into a national sector recognized and funded as such for the first time, that colleges even came together under the umbrella of one Association of Colleges. The competitive conditions under which they now exist make it easy and tempting for colleges to divide and squabble amongst themselves in desperate struggles for survival, typically blaming one another as the devil takes the hindmost. This occurred, for instance, in response to the sudden threat from government to cut the Demand Led Element of funding in February 1997, when the colleges were unable to present a united front to argue their case.

Despite all the talk about education during that campaign, attention was once again centred upon schools. We also heard a lot of unfocused rhetoric from politicians and pundits about 'the learning society' of 'lifelong learners' that was presented by all parties as so vital, not only to economic prosperity but to social cohesion. In the 1997 General Election it was clear that whichever party won, a high priority in education for the new government would be what to do about the crisis of the colleges.

The least that could be done would be to institute, immediately, a review of further education as far-reaching as the Dearing Review of Higher Education. This would urgently examine the workings of the FEFC funding method, and its consequences for colleges. A national inquiry would also look towards frameworks for institutional co-operation based in and responsive to their local communities. This demands thinking in terms of the regionalized learning infrastructure we have advocated. Curricular reform is no less urgent and here we have looked to what we called 'a Scottish solution' as an initial step forward. This requires a coherent framework of academic and vocational qualifications with built-in transfer and progression. Equitable finance for *all* students, in further as well as higher education, must also be instituted to end long-standing anomalies and alleviate student poverty. These are just a few of the many pressing issues for urgent consideration. Until the report of such an inquiry, of the type that NATFHE is now calling for, policy should be consolidated to establish a proper base and rationale for expansion.

Yet it is predictable that, once again, higher education – facing its own, linked but not quite so immediate and severe, crisis of funding and purpose – will steal the limelight as Dearing reports to donnish dissension and political applause in the summer of 1997. Meanwhile, unnoticed, the much more severe and immediate crisis of the FE colleges will continue, affecting far larger numbers of staff and students. Dearing's is the second major report on higher education following Robbins in 1963 and there have been several reports on schools. No similar inquiry has been held into non-university, post-compulsory education since Crowther in 1959 and nothing on technical education since the Samuelson Commission in 1884. The concentration upon abstract and selective, academic study, to the neglect of the applied and vocational, is widely acknowledged to be the bane of English education. It is linked through the status and snobbery of 'Official Knowledge' to an outmoded class system. With every politician's rhetoric elevating education to its present unprecedented position at the top of the national agenda, the future of learning other than the academic has to be faced along with that of the FE colleges which have preserved and developed practical skills together with generalized knowledge.

We have suggested that this valuing of knowledge and skills other than, or as well as, the abstract and academic, challenges the existing hierarchy in society between those who think and those who do. Yet we have also argued that this is the wider challenge to society made by the latest applications of new communication and information technologies. Ultimately, this new technology offers the prospect of so changing the nature of work as to overcome the division between mental and manual labour, widening genuine access to all and affording everyone opportunities to contribute to society through full if not full-time employment. Learning need not then be tied only to earning but to leisure and to encouraging active participation in public life. Indeed, questions of democratic participation are inseparable from those concerning the future of the welfare state as a whole, of which education is but one part. In the end, it is only through a resolute democratization that the future of the welfare state can be secured and the trend towards relentless commercialization and privatization administered by the quangos of the Contracting State can be reversed.

These are larger questions than those concerning the further education colleges alone. Yet FE has an essential contribution to make to this long-term viable future for society, particularly in preserving and developing knowledges and skills whose value and use are too often unrecognized. In order for the colleges to play their part in future economic and social progress, their immediate future has to be secured. We hope that this book has helped to draw attention to the urgency of this task.

References and bibliography

Introduction

Bilston College Publications have published a number of books by various authors in
association with *Education Now* (from whom they are available c/o 113 Arundel
Drive, Bramcote Hills, Nottingham). Frank Reeves *The Modernity of Further
Education* (referred to in Chapter 6) was published by them in 1995 and his book
with Anna Frankel on *The FE Curriculum* (referred to in the Introduction) was
published in 1996.

On the learning society, see the European Union White Paper on 'Education and
Training, Teaching and Learning, Towards the Learning Society', available on the
internet or from Brussels. Also, Stewart Ranson *Towards the Learning Society* and
his *Inside the Learning Society*, Cassell 1994 and 1997. Cassell also published
Cantor, Roberts and Pratley's latest version of their *A Guide to Further Education
in England and Wales* in 1995. Gleeson, Mardle and McCourt's 1980 *Further
Education or Training? A case study in the theory and practice of day-release
education* was published by Routledge.

The government reports and White Papers we refer to are available from HMSO, or the
relevant departments and agencies, e.g. the DfEE in the case of Dearing's Reviews,
the DTI for the Competitiveness White Papers and the former ED and
MSC/Training Agency for their publications (now lodged with the DfEE). FEFC
documents are obtainable directly from them in Coventry, just as NCVQ
publications, like Dr Capey's 'GNVQ: Assessment Report' 1995, or Gordon
Beaumont's 1996 review of NVQs and SVQS, are available from what is now the
Qualifications and Curriculum Authority (QCA).

Peter Winch's *The Idea of a Social Science and its Relation to Philosophy* is a standard
work first published by Routledge in 1958.

Chapter 1

The history of further and technical education in the UK is still to be written, however
Brian Simon's monumental four-volume *Studies in the History of Education* cover
the years from 1780 to 1994 and are published by Lawrence and Wishart. Andy
Green's *Education and State Formation*, Macmillan 1990, compares the rise of
education systems in England, France and the USA, though, like even Simon,
'education systems' are rather restricted to schools. More recent history of training
is covered by Brendan Evans' *Politics of the Training Market* (Routledge 1993),
while Ainley and Corney's *Training for the Future, the Rise and Fall of the MSC*

(Cassell 1990) remains the only history of the Manpower Services Commission.

Caroline Benn and Clyde Chitty's epic survey *Thirty Years On: Is Comprehensive Education Alive and Well or Struggling to Survive?* (David Fulton 1996: Penguin) covers the 30 years since their first survey with Brian Simon first published in 1970 and this time includes responses from the FE sector.

For sixth-form colleges, see Eric Macfarlane's 1993 Routledge-published *Education 16–19 in Transition.*

Eric Robinson's *The New Polytechnics, the People's Universities* was published as a Penguin in 1968, while Peter Scott's *The Meanings of Mass Higher Education* is published by the Open University Press in association with the Society for Research in Higher Education. John Pratt has recently written a detailed record of what he calls *The Polytechnic Experiment 1965–1992* (Open University Press, 1997) but his first report on the polytechnics with Tyrrell Burgess (referred to on page 2) was published by Pitman in 1974.

The journal article referred to by Denis Gleeson is 'Legislating for Change: Missed Opportunities in the Further and Higher Education Act' in *The British Journal of Education and Work*, Vol. 6, No. 2, 1996.

A comprehensive background statistical picture attractively presented of 'Further Education in the Market Place' – as it is subtitled – can be found in *Changing Colleges* by Alan Smithers and Pamela Robinson, though since it was published by the Council for Industry and Higher Education in 1993, it is rather out of date. Perhaps they will soon update it. In the meantime, FEFC annual reports and other publications present similar information, though not always all in one place.

Kenneth Baker's autobiography *The Turbulent Years: My Life in Politics* was published in London by Faber in 1993.

Chapter 2

Lewisham College has published a series of 'Praxis Papers', written by members of staff and, like Bilston's publications, printed and distributed at the college's own expense. Two of them which inform the discussion of funding and its effects presented here are No. 2 *Towards a Nation of Shopkeepers; the vocationalizing of the FE curriculum* by Derek Frampton, published in 1995, and No. 4, published in 1996, *ISR; Institutional Surveillance and 'so-called data'* by Julian Gravatt and Ian Pert.

Alison Wolf has written a very clear exposition of *Competence-Based Assessment* (Open University Press 1994). Phil Hodkinson and Mary Issitt (eds) examine *The Challenge of Competence* (Cassell 1995). Peter Robinson's *Rhetoric and Reality, Britain's New Vocational Qualifications* (Centre for Economic Performance, London School of Economics 1996) reveals the reality of its implementation. The important Audit Commission/OFSTED report 'Unfinished Business: Full-time Evaluation Courses for 16–19-year-olds' was published in 1993 by HMSO.

Artifex Semper Anxilio: A century of Vocational Education in South East London is by Roy Bowne and Peter Latham, published by Alan Sulton 1991.

Chapter 3

Of the books on 'The Management of Further Education' their name is legion, however we can recommend one new one with that title (subtitled 'Theory and Practice') by Harriet Harper (David Fulton 1997).

Alan Greer and Paul Hoggett's 'Steering Between Government and the Market: the Governance of Local Spending Bodies' is a report to the Rowntree Foundation 1997.

Chapter 5

Bob Coles' *Youth and Social Policy: Youth Citizenship and Youth Careers* (London UCL Press, 1995) helps to conceptualize the situation of young people today and relates it to the neglected issue of citizenship, as does Gill Jones and Claire Wallace's *Youth, Family and Citizenship* (Open University Press 1992).

An interesting report on 'First Generation Stayers-On' in schools and at college was published by Norwich College in association with Norfolk LEA's Educational Press. 'Sixth Form Options' by Sandie Schagen, Fiona Johnson and Clare Simkin of the National Foundation for Educational Research reviewed the choices facing students in 'post-compulsory education in maintained schools' in 1996. In the same year Jane Hemsley-Brown completed an unpublished Ph.D. thesis on 'Marketing Post-Sixteen Colleges' at the University of Southampton which points to the importance for colleges and schools of their 'image' in the minds of their 'consumers'. Having got them into college, the retention of students on their courses is, we have seen, an important priority for colleges; however, a Widening Participation Committee chaired by Helena Kennedy QC reported in July 1997 on how to get more students now that participation by 16–19-year-olds has peaked, directing colleges instead towards adult students.

There are several books on special needs in FE but Jenny Corbett and Len Barton's *A Struggle for Choice, Students with Special Needs in Transition to Adulthood* (Routledge 1992) can be commended along with Jean McGinty and John Fish's *Further Education in the Market Place, Equity, Opportunity and Individual Learning* (Routledge 1993), plus the 1996 'Report of the Learning Difficulties and/or Disabilities Committee' (the Tomlinson Report) for the FEFC on 'Inclusive Learning'. Jenny Corbett writes about 'losing labels' in *Bad Mouthing, The Language of Special Needs* (Falmer Press 1996).

Chapter 6

Vince Hall's *Maintained Further Education in the United Kingdom* was published by the Further Education Staff College in 1990 with a new edition in 1994.

The Further Education Unit's 'A Basis for Credit, a post-16 credit and accumulation transfer framework' was published by them in 1992. FEU also published 'A basis for choice: report of a study group on post-16 pre-employment courses' in 1979.

David Robertson *et al.* (1994) 'Choosing to Change, Extending Access, Choice and Mobility in Higher Education: the Report of the HEQC CAT Development Project', London: Higher Education Quality Council. Also on HE: Patrick Ainley

Degrees of Difference, Higher Education in the 1990s, Lawrence and Wishart 1994.

The London-based Institute for Public Policy Research *A British Baccalaureate: Ending the Division Between Education and Training* was published in 1990. Looking to 'Dearing and Beyond', Ann Hodgson and Ken Spours examine *14–19 Qualifications, Frameworks and Systems* in an edited collection published by Kogan Page 1997. Geoff Stanton also has relevant proposals in his 1996 report on 'Output Related Funding and the Quality of Education and Training', available from the International Centre for Research on Assessment at the London University Institute of Education.

NATFHE discusses 'The Future Organisation of Post-School Education and Training' in a 1994 paper and the Union's General Education Section has collaborated with the National Union of Teachers to write a discussion document in 1994 on '14–19 Education: The Way Forward', while the Socialist Teachers' Alliance also contributed to the debate on the future of education policy with 'Reforming 14 – 19 Education: What New Labour *Could* Do' (1996). 'A Radical Look at Education Today and a Strategy for the Future' are also to be found in 'Learning to Succeed', the 1993 report of the Paul Hamlyn Foundation.

For London, *The Strategic Planning of Further Education, Widening the Debate* was published by the Association of London Government in 1997.

Stanley Aronowitz and William DiFazio's *The Jobless Future, Sci-tech and the Dogma of Work* (University of Minnesota Press, 1994) is the latest to a long line of discussion on the effects of new communications and informations technology on the labour process. Patrick Ainley's *Class and Skill, Changing Divisions of Knowledge and Labour* (Cassell 1993) relates some of this debate to the social situation in the UK.

Mike Cooley's remarks are to be found in his paper 'Skill and Competence for the 21st Century' given to the IITD 24th National Conference held in Galway in 1993, as is the quote from James Joyes with which we preface the chapter.

Appendix

The questionnaire used as the basis for semi-structured interviews with students

---

Personal information

M/F

Age

Ethnicity (Would you describe yourself as a member of an ethnic/national minority?)

Disability (Would you describe yourself as having a disability?)

Parents' occupations F/M

Siblings

Partner/Boyfriend/Girlfriend

Children/dependents

If you have stated 'Yes' to the above questions: Do you have any commitments to your family/partner/dependents that take up your time to the extent of affecting your work at college? Or do your parents/partner support you (financially or otherwise) through college?

Have you had to take time off from college for any other reasons, e.g. health?

Previous education and employment history

Qualifications
(gained at school and college, to date)

Work
(Provide details of any full-time positions held, as well as part-time work carried out during term time including the number of hours per week:

Does your work interfere with your college work?

Income

Have you taken out/applied for a:
- student loan
- grant
- discretionary award
- educational bursary
- access fund
- income support
- unemployment benefit
- severe hardship payments
- bank or other loan?

Is this enough to pay for college requirements (fees, transport, books and equipment, residentials/visits, social activities associated with the college, including eating properly)?

Full-time/Part-time study courses
(shortened – as SOC, PSY, ENG etc.)

Selection of courses and college:

Was Home Counties/Inner City your first choice, second etc. choices (if any)?

Is/are the course(s) you are following your first choice?

Have you changed course or are you considering doing so (including leaving the college)?

What qualifications did you have to have to get on this course?

Why did you decided to enter FE rather than staying at school or going to work?

How did you find out about the college:
* parents
* other members of family
* friends
* teachers
* careers officer
* advertising
* other

Experience

Has FE met your expectations? (Re. adequacy of information and guidance for courses.)

Is it a rewarding experience?

If 'yes' is this because of:
* interest in subject
* and/or other things you do in college

Anticipated qualifications

Knowledge and skills

As a result of study and/or college generally:
Have you learnt a lot of information /knowledge?

Acquired
- practical skills
- social skills
- 'core'/'key' skills (including IT)?

Has your study made you think differently (about things in general/your subject in particular)?

Have you made new friends?

Social background

Would you call yourself working class, middle class or any other class, or don't you think of yourself like that?

Other students: What would you say was the social (class) background of other students at your college? (Does this vary by course/faculty?)

Has your college experience increased your confidence?

Attitude to work

Numbers of hours in classes/labs per week:
Number of hours in:
- private study at college and at home
- the library/research
- collective study

Do students support each other or are they competitive?

Is this:

- too much work
- too little
- about right?

How much time do you spend

- writing
- in taught sessions (listening/taking notes)
- discussing topics
- private study/homework

How large are your classes?
Have many people left your course? Why?

How does college compare to school:

- Do the lecturers (/teachers) treat you as adults (Cf. adult students/first name terms)?
- Can you ask them about anything you don't understand without feeling stupid?
- Pace of teaching.
- Quality of teaching.
- Is this the right level of course for you?

How useful are tutorials:

- personal
- subject

Have you used the:

- careers service
- student counsellor
- students' union (are you a member?)

and were they helpful?

Is the college in general responsive to your demands?
Do you think this is because they really care about you and/or for other reasons?

Does your course offer work experience?
If yes, was this part of the attraction of the course? Was it useful?
If no, should there have been some form of work experience?

Future

Will more opportunities be open to you in employment as a result of your study?
Is this the reason you are taking this course(s)?

Do you plan to undertake any further training/study?
Type of occupation desired:

Expected salary:

Type of employer sought in employment:
- public/private
- large/small
- UK/non-UK
- self-employment

Are you looking for full-time/part-time work?

Would you seek to move between organizations or stay in one place and 'work your way up'? (flexible careers)

What is the highest position you aspire to?

What is your definition of/Do you think of yourself as 'having a career'?

Do you think you will be treated on your merits by potential employers in the job market or do you anticipate being discriminated against for any reason?

Personal future

Where do you see yourself in:
- 5 years?
- 10 years?

Which of the following are most important to you:

- home
- work
- other

Do you expect your partner (if you anticipate having one) to pursue her/his own career?

Interests and activities

Please provide details of:
- social/political activities
- community activities
- leisure/recreation activities

Britain's future

Do you think things in general will get better or worse?

How do you intend to vote in local/national elections and how have you voted in the past (if you have)?

Housing

Where do you live now (name of town/district)?
Is your accommodation:
- privately owned
- privately rented
- public rented (council or housing association)

If you don't live with your parents, when did you first leave your parents' home?

Costs of housing (including any contribution to parents)

Where do you plan to live in future?

Do you have access to:

a word-processor/computer?

your own room?

What do you use as means of transport?

Miscellaneous

What holidays do you take, if any?

Estimated expenditure per week: £

Do you have any savings?

Any other comments:

The literal transcriptions of the interviews from this questionnaire have been archived anonymously, together with the authors' interviews with HE students. All information is held at the Economic and Social Research Council's Qualitative Data Archive at Essex University, and is available for use by other students and their teachers.

Index

with acronyms of key terms/bodies